IMAGES
of America

IMMACULATE HEART
OF MARY SISTERS
OF MICHIGAN

Patricia Montemurri

Here is an aerial view of the Sisters, Servants of the Immaculate Heart of Mary (IHM) Motherhouse, built in 1931–1932. It is located in the southeastern Michigan town of Monroe at 610 West Elm Avenue, along the River Raisin. The IHM congregation was established in a log cabin along the river in 1845 and is Michigan's oldest institute of Catholic women religious. (Courtesy of Sisters, Servants of the Immaculate Heart of Mary Archives.)

On the Cover: Dozens of IHM Sisters line the Motherhouse's brick-arched hallway for a 1945 photograph. They were not allowed to speak to each other while waiting to enter the dining hall. It once was discouraged for IHM Sisters to be photographed, but 1945 marked the congregation's 100th anniversary, and the centennial occasioned some rare newspaper coverage. (Courtesy of Sisters, Servants of the Immaculate Heart of Mary Archives.)

IMAGES
of America

IMMACULATE HEART OF MARY SISTERS OF MICHIGAN

Patricia Montemurri

ARCADIA
PUBLISHING

Published by Arcadia Publishing
Charleston, South Carolina

Printed in the United States of America

Library of Congress Control Number: 2019945974

For all general information, please contact Arcadia Publishing:
Telephone 843-853-2070
Fax 843-853-0044
E-mail sales@arcadiapublishing.com
For customer service and orders:
Toll-Free 1-888-313-2665

Visit us on the Internet at www.arcadiapublishing.com

*In memory of my parents, Nanda and Mario Montemurri,
who sent my sister, Donna, and me to St. Thomas Aquinas
Catholic School in Detroit, staffed by the Monroe IHMs.*

CONTENTS

Acknowledgments   6

Introduction   7

1.   Foundation   11

2.   Taking the Veil   21

3.   Motherhouse Memories   31

4.   Breaking Ground in Education   41

5.   Classroom Lessons   51

6.   Faith in Change and Prayer   71

7.   Where There Is a Need   83

8.   The Sustainable Motherhouse   93

9.   IHMs in Action Today   101

Bibliography   126

About the Sisters, Servants of the Immaculate Heart of Mary   127

ACKNOWLEDGMENTS

Long before I joined the staff of the *Detroit Free Press*, the first newspaper I worked on was my own. It was reported, edited, and glued together for a third-grade assignment from Sister Archange Groh at St. Thomas Aquinas Elementary School on Detroit's far west side. Sister Archange was an IHM, a member of the blue-robed Sisters, Servants of the Immaculate Heart of Mary of Monroe, Michigan. My grade school was staffed by them. She told my Italian immigrant parents that I had a knack for writing.

When I was in fifth grade, I got a behind-the-scenes glimpse of the changes underway among American Catholic nuns after the Second Vatican Council reforms. Many Catholic women religious had chosen to shed their congregation's full-length and veiled habits (based on designs dating back to the Middle Ages) to wear more modern attire. Sister Archange was one of them. She visited our home so that my mother, a seamstress, could shorten her habit. She also asked mom to help touch up the gray in her curly bangs, which would be publicly revealed for the first time in decades as she donned a shorter, modified veil.

My academics also were influenced by other IHM teachers, including Sister Marguerite (Ann Philip) Daly in fourth grade and Sister Alice (Theotilda) O'Hara in seventh grade. Under Sister Therese (James Marie) Kearney, a music teacher, I mastered the alto harmony of "Battle Hymn of the Republic." And in my Catholic high school, Sister Susan Rakoczy and former IHM Moni McIntyre, now an Episcopalian priest and an IHM Associate, were beloved religion teachers. As a *Detroit Free Press* journalist, I wrote about the IHMs and Catholic issues, and the late Sisters Carol (Laura) Quigley and Barbara Johns were helpful sources.

Special thanks to the unending patience of the IHM Archives staff: director Jennifer Meacham, Sister Diann (Bernard Therese) Cousino, and Deborah Saul, writer of *Today and Yesterday*, an IHM Archives quarterly.

Copies of the now-discontinued *IHM Archives Notes*, created by retired archivist Donna Westley and Sister Anne (Anne Jerome) Crane, were indispensable.

Thank you also to the IHM Leadership Council, Sisters Mary Jane Herb, Marianne Gaynor, Patricia (Ann Bernard) McCluskey, Margaret Chapman, and Ellen Rinke. Thank you to Sister Maxine Kollasch. IHM communications director Molly Hunt deserves a special thank you because of her good humor and ability to answer questions. Thank you to Michaela Kotanova.

Thank you also to my Arcadia Publishing editor, Caitrin Cunningham, who has indulged, nudged, and encouraged me now through three Arcadia Publishing books involving Catholics in Detroit. Many thanks to Arcadia Publishing editor Sara Miller for her patient and meticulous review. Thank you also to photographer Diane Weiss and Kathy Kieliszewski, *Detroit Free Press* director of photo and video.

When applicable and when space allows, IHM Sisters are identified with both their religious names and the birth names many resumed using after the Second Vatican Council reforms of the 1960s. Unless otherwise noted, the photographs in this book come from the rich archives of the Sisters, Servants of the Immaculate Heart of Mary in Monroe and the IHM Communications Office.

INTRODUCTION

Sister Lynne Moldenhauer can still hear the first whisper of a call to religious life. It happened when she was four. Seated with her family in the pews of Holy Cross Catholic Church in Marine City, Michigan, she was transfixed by the sisters who staffed the parish school as they filed in for Sunday morning Mass. They wore royal blue habits then, contrasted against blazing white wimples and black veils. They were nicknamed the "Blue Nuns," but formally, they were the Sisters, Servants of the Immaculate Heart of Mary, or the IHMs.

"I was so intrigued that I got up from my family and went and sat with them," Sister Lynne recalls. The IHMs, based in Monroe, Michigan, were her teachers from first grade through her time at Detroit's Marygrove College. Inspired by them, she decided to become an IHM and entered the congregation in 1973. Sister Lynne's first IHM ministry was in a women's shelter in South Carolina—a big departure from the traditional teaching jobs of IHMs and a sign of changing times for women religious.

Something went awry in her first years in South Carolina, she says. She left the IHMs in 1979, eventually becoming a South Carolina probation and parole officer. But, she says, "I never ended my relationship with the IHMs. Even though I left, I never left in my heart."

So, she was following her heart when she rejoined the congregation in 2016, becoming coordinator of the IHMs' Maxis Spirituality Center, a retreat complex in the Detroit suburb of Riverview.

"They really took me under their wings and loved me into being. I knew that this was the life God was calling me to," Sister Lynne explains. Her IHM mentors have been "kind, compassionate, prayerful, and faithful servants of the Gospel," she says, and it's "how I wanted to be in the world."

In 2020, as the Monroe IHMs celebrate the 175th anniversary of their founding, the oldest established congregation of Catholic religious women in Michigan continues to welcome new members. The IHM mission has evolved to meet pressing needs of today, reverberating in the congregation's assertive commitment to social justice, environmental sustainability, and prayerful spirituality.

American congregations of sisters and nuns swelled last century, in part, because many members came from large immigrant families, and women had fewer options for education or careers. At the congregation's peak, around 1960, there were some 1,600 sisters staffing some 100 grade schools, high schools, and colleges throughout Michigan and other states. For decades, the IHM mission was associated with classroom education. Today, there are still IHMs who work in schools and colleges in the United States and overseas, but there is no longer an IHM teaching in an elementary school classroom in the Detroit area or in the IHMs' hometown of Monroe. The congregation faces profound challenges, as do most US congregations of Catholic religious. At the end of 2019, the IHMs numbered about 265 with an average age of 79. In 2019, three women took vows to join the congregation; in the 1950s, the annual classes of new sisters numbered in the sixties.

IHMs have taught an estimated 700,000 students since 1845, among them business and government luminaries, television and rock stars, and civic and religious leaders. One of them, Kaye Lani Rae Rafko, became Miss America 1988—the first registered nurse to win the title. At Detroit Holy Redeemer, they taught Jack White of the White Stripes and "Seven Nation Army" fame. At Monroe St. Mary Elementary School, the students included National Public Radio (NPR) national political correspondent Don Gonyea. IHMs taught a lion of Congress, the late Rep. John Dingell, and a prince of the Church, Detroit-bred Cardinal Joseph Tobin of Newark, New Jersey.

Starting in 1927, the IHMs operated Marygrove College in Detroit. It opened as an all-women's college and became coed in 1971, educating scores of teachers, social workers, artists, dancers, and musicians. But the college was beset by high costs, deep deficits, and declining enrollment. These factors have caused the closing or consolidation of about two dozen private US liberal arts colleges since 2016. Sadly, Marygrove has joined the list after closing on December 31, 2019. However, the IHMs have collaborated with several organizations to preserve the 53-acre campus as a place for learning. The IHMs have deeded the campus to the Marygrove Conservancy, principally funded by the Michigan-based Kresge Foundation. Kresge has committed $50 million to transforming Marygrove into a "cradle-to-career" campus, offering education from preschool to community college, and has partnered with the Detroit Public Schools Community District, the University of Michigan, and Starfish Family Services.

IHMs continue to educate in other ways.

"We are enriched by our past and look forward to our future," says Sister Mary Jane Herb, the IHM president. "While we will be a smaller community, the IHM mission will live on in the future. Our efforts will continue to reach out to women called to religious life."

Today's IHMs are involved in a variety of ministries. They work running parishes, as court-appointed guardians, as communications professionals, and as leaders of nonprofit organizations and spiritual counselors. Long ago, women entered the convent straight out of high school. The newest IHMs bring talents from real-world experience. They've discerned a calling over years of reflection and prayer while experiencing the bumps and bruises of life. And in the digital age, IHM Sisters are pioneers.

When Sister Julie Vieira became an IHM in 2006, she was in her mid-30s and the youngest member of the congregation. As she prepared for her vows, she started a blog titled *A Nun's Life*. She shared her rich spiritual quest to join the IHMs with readers from around the world, answering questions about everything from the differences between religious congregations to her favorite beers. Sister Julie and IHM Sister Maxine Kollasch cofounded A Nun's Life Ministry; its website (ANunsLife.org) features stories, videos, and blogs and recently exceeded more than one million downloaded podcasts.

It has been a half century since most IHMs wore floor-length habits and veils. Today, all but one of them do their ministries in street clothes. They were known for their blue habits, but they are now associated with being ecologically green. Their 376,000-square-foot Monroe Motherhouse, built during the Depression, was renovated in 2003 with energy efficiency and renewable resources at the forefront. It has become a national model for green building projects, earning awards from the US Environmental Protection Agency.

IHM president Sister Mary Jane contrasted the congregation's past and future in an address she delivered on November 9, 2019, as the IHMs began their 175th anniversary year:

"We are dealing with political challenges—not building a house, but rather renovating one. Not staffing a school, but ensuring that our sponsored ministries continue," she said. "The new life, perhaps our resurrected life, takes the form of addressing the issues of climate change, dealing with racism, struggling with what it means to be a member of the Church who faces significant challenges today. We celebrate that new life and commit ourselves to engage in establishing our new narrative."

The IHMs emphatically make it clear that they are sisters who want to impact their communities. In the public's mind, the terms nuns and sisters are used interchangeably. But by Roman Catholic definition, a nun generally lives a life of contemplation in a cloister cut off from public engagement. Both nuns and sisters take vows of poverty, celibacy, and obedience. In contrast, a Catholic sister serves among the public.

The IHMs say their activism was inherent from the time of the congregation's founding in 1845. Rev. Louis Gillet and Sister Theresa Maxis Duchemin opened a school on the River Raisin's banks to educate girls. Sister Theresa was the out-of-wedlock daughter of a mixed-race Haitian refugee and a British military officer. Fluent in French, she could pass for white, and Reverend Gillet recruited her to teach French-Canadian Catholic settlers in Monroe. Before she arrived in

Monroe, she became an early member of the Oblate Sisters of Providence in Baltimore, the first US congregation for women of color. After establishing the Monroe IHMs, Sister Theresa also founded two more IHM congregations in Pennsylvania, both separate from the Michigan branch. Because of her mixed-race heritage and gender, she encountered prejudice from church officials, who sought to minimize her impact and ostracize her (for a time) from the three communities she founded.

Sister Theresa Maxis heroically responded to the needs of the day, notes Sister Maxine Kollasch, and "her struggles reflected a society and a world crying out for social justice in the midst of oppression. It is her 175-year legacy of service, perseverance, visionary ideas and trust in God's providence that is being celebrated today."

Here is a sampling of notable Monroe IHM activism over the years:

- The IHMs helped avert a 1934 Monroe bank collapse using a strategy devised by IHM Sr. Miriam Raymo, the congregation's business manager. She and several other sisters stood in long lines at the bank. "They were commissioned to deposit a quarter at a time and then go back to the end of the line and to talk to as many people as possible, trying to build confidence that the bank would not fail," notes an IHM account. It didn't.
- The IHMs were at the forefront of the Sister Formation movement, which pushed for religious sisters to get college degrees before becoming Catholic classroom teachers. At the heart of the movement was the conviction that professional teacher preparation was key to providing the best education possible for Catholic students. However, some bishops initially opposed it, because Catholic officials had to hire lay teachers, who were far more expensive, to fill the void left by sisters taking longer to complete their studies.
- In 1971, IHM Sisters resigned from St. Raymond Elementary School on Detroit's east side to protest parish families resisting racial integration.
- The IHMs became activist stockholders to urge Detroit Edison, now known as DTE Energy, to provide better safety measures for workers at the Fermi II nuclear reactor. Sister Amata Miller spoke out at shareholder meetings in the 1970s.
- IHMs have run an AIDS hospice in South Africa, worked for human rights in El Salvador, lived with the poor of Honduras, and taught in Uganda during the reign of dictator Idi Amin. They help asylum-seekers and refugees at the Mexico border.
- For decades, the IHM's Marygrove College in Detroit hosted the weekly Mass by Dignity, an association of gay Catholics. Even though Marygrove College has closed, the weekly Dignity Mass in Marygrove's Sacred Heart Chapel will continue.

The IHMs struggle, too, with divisive issues that have impacted other Catholic organizations, such as the Church's treatment of LGBT employees. Because of the congregation's progressive track record, there was an outcry in 2014, when the IHM-sponsored Marian High School in suburban Detroit fired a chemistry teacher—a lesbian whose pregnancy through in vitro fertilization was against Catholic teachings. Without going into details about the firing, IHM president Sister Mary Jane Herb says the IHMs are exploring ways to deal with similar situations in the future. From 2007 through 2019, about 90 Catholic Church employees have been fired over issues of sexuality and marriage, according to New Ways Ministry.

The IHMs don't shy away from controversial causes. In July 2019, at the annual Jubilee Mass honoring IHMs celebrating milestone anniversaries of ministry, IHM Sr. Barbara Stanbridge extended a few challenges. "In this year of Jubilee, can we reinvigorate ourselves by bringing sight to the blind, to those blinded by racism, sexism and classism? Can we help the lame walk, whether it's our sisters on walkers or those who are taking the long road to freedom?" Sister Barbara asked. She questioned the Catholic Church's opposition to legal same-sex marriage and a priesthood limited to unmarried men. "To our Church, can we say people want to get married regardless of their sexual orientation?" Sister Barbara said, also adding that "some will soon not have Eucharist because we have limited the priesthood."

This book gives but a glimpse of the contributions of Monroe IHMs over the decades. Sister Ambrosia Fitzgerald was one of the first women to earn a doctorate in physics at the University of Michigan. While teaching high school science in Detroit, she was recruited to secretly work on the Manhattan Project, which led to the development of the atomic weapons used during World War II. From the suffering of Sister Catherine Frances Mallon, doctors extracted cancerous breast tissue cells that exponentially grew into a research line used in 25,000 cited experiments and was responsible for treatment breakthroughs. The success of the cell line wasn't credited to miracles, but the sister's contribution has been dubbed "immortal."

IHM Sisters are groundbreaking theologians and have been national leaders among US women religious. Four IHMs have been elected president of the Leadership Conference of Women Religious (LCWR), an organization representing the majority of US sisters and nuns. Sister Sharon (Marie Russell) Holland, a canon lawyer and one of the highest-ranking female officials in a 21-year career at the Vatican, was key in resolving bitter disputes between the Vatican and American sisters. In 2014 and 2015, Sister Sharon helped end long-running Vatican investigations into the LCWR and of US congregations of sisters and nuns.

Today, many IHMs identify as feminists. Their founders didn't know that word, but they were protofeminists, "laying the foundation for feminism," says Margaret Susan Thompson, a Syracuse University associate professor of history and women's studies. Thompson studies the evolution of American women religious through a feminist perspective and contributed to the 1997 book *Building Sisterhood*, which features essays that explore the IHMs' legacy in the context of women's rights and a male-run Catholic Church. Thompson is now an IHM Associate—an initiative for lay women and men to study with an IHM mentor to share in the congregation's life and ministry.

Some Catholics taught by IHM Sisters are not happy with them now and wish they still wore habits and were more conservative in their public policy pursuits, notes Thompson. But "the IHMs don't do what they're doing instead of prayer," says Thompson. "They do it because of prayer and faith. Faith girds everything that they do."

The newest IHM is Sister Jane Aseltyne, who made her first vows at the age of 34 on August 4, 2019, at the Monroe Motherhouse. She was raised an evangelical Christian, but two of her great-aunts had joined the IHMs, siblings Sisters Patricia (Helen Mary) and Ann (Ann Arthur) Aseltyne. At a family gathering in 2011, Jane talked to her aunts about her work with at-risk youth and senior citizens. Jane told her aunt Pat about wrestling with what her future might hold.

"I spent six months asking God what God wanted from me," Sister Jane recounted. "I wanted a life of simplicity. I wanted to be in a place rooted in the Gospel call." From her purse, Jane showed her aunts the book she was reading: the prayers of St. Teresa of Avila.

"She's a patron saint of the IHMs," Sister Patricia told her. "I'll be in touch."

When Jane visited the IHM Motherhouse, "I felt like a met a lot of people who spoke a similar God language."

She converted to Catholicism and worked with A Nun's Life Ministry. Her vocation isn't rooted in Hollywood's portrayal of women religious in movies like *The Sound of Music* and *Sister Act* or the grade-school memories of so many Catholic baby boomers. She realizes her calling sparks curiosity—even animosity.

"I haven't been coerced or brainwashed. I have been called by God. Religious life provides me with a community, and it's not something I pick and choose when to live it," says Sister Jane. "I choose it every day. It's coming from within me, and it's the gift I have to serve the world."

One

FOUNDATION

In 1845, Sr. Theresa Maxis Duchemin arrived in Monroe in southeastern Michigan. She was born out of wedlock in 1810 in Baltimore as Marie Almaide Maxis Duchemin. Her mother was a Haitian refugee of mixed race and a servant for a well-to-do Haitian family, the Duchemins. Her father was a British military officer and a Duchemin family friend. She attended a Baltimore boarding school for Haitians. At age 19, she joined the Oblate Sisters of Providence of Baltimore, the world's first religious order for women of color. In Baltimore, Sister Theresa met Rev. Louis Florent Gillet, a Belgian-born Redemptorist doing missionary work in Michigan. Gillet wanted to open a school for French-Canadian settlers in Monroe and recruited Theresa because she was proficient in French and English. Light-skinned and blue-eyed, Theresa passed for white upon her arrival in Monroe in September 1845. On November 10, 1845, she and Gillet established a religious congregation for women called the Sisters of Providence. Two years later, the name was changed to the Sisters, Servants of the Immaculate Heart of Mary (IHM). This drawing depicts her as an IHM.

11

Rev. Louis Florent Gillet was born in Antwerp, Belgium, in 1813 and entered the Redemptorist order of priests in 1832. Gillet left Europe in 1843 and visited Michigan as a missionary to fledgling Detroit-area parishes. When he became pastor at St. Mary Parish in Monroe, he sought sisters to open a school. In Baltimore, he met Sr. Theresa Maxis, and they cofounded the Monroe IHMs. "If I cannot find a religious community, I will make one," he wrote. He died in France in 1892. His remains are interred in the Father Gillet Memorial Chapel at the IHMs' St. Mary Cemetery in Monroe. "I desire to be everywhere when I see so many needs," Gillet said of his missionary work in a statement that has rooted the IHMs' mission.

The first two women to join Sr. Theresa Maxis in Monroe were Charlotte Shaaff and Theresa Renauld. Shaaff came to know Sister Theresa because both had been members of the Oblate Sisters of Providence congregation in Baltimore. Shaaff also was of mixed-race heritage and took the religious name of Sister Anne Constance; later, she was known as Sister Ann. In his missionary travels around Michigan, Rev. Louis Florent Gillet had met Renauld, a young churchgoer at the parish now known as St. Paul on the Lake in Grosse Pointe, east of Detroit. Her parents had donated land for the parish's first church, where she heard Gillet preach in 1843. She became Sister Celestine and is pictured here.

This rendering depicts the log cabin where the first IHM Sisters lived. Another small house nearby was used as the first school, the Young Ladies Academy, which opened in January 1846. It was the forerunner of St. Mary Academy. The school enrolled 40 students, including four boarders. The sisters' log cabin home, Sister Celestine wrote, "was filled with life and light and love which no darkness overshadowed, no desolation made drear."

This wood-frame addition to the IHM convent was built by Rev. Egidius Smulders in 1851; he had replaced Father Gillet as the congregation's overseer. In 1869, the sisters left it for the first Motherhouse, and the building later served as the school for Monroe St. Mary Parish until 1910.

This is the only known photograph of Sr. Theresa Maxis, taken in 1867, but she was not wearing the IHM habit. She was fervent in her deep faith, and her missionary zeal led to conflicts with Catholic bishops. There is evidence that scorn for her mixed-race heritage fueled the conflicts. She particularly clashed with Detroit bishop Peter Paul Lefevere. Lefevere came to Monroe in 1858 to upbraid her. "I got his blessing as usual; then he reproached me for being headstrong and selfwilled. I knelt down," she wrote. A few days later, Lefevere commanded her to Pennsylvania, where she established IHM congregations in Scranton and near Philadelphia. In Michigan, Sister Theresa had been replaced by Mother Mary Joseph Walker, who displayed a rigid leadership style. "This shift in leadership created significant tension within the very fabric of the community," Sr. Barbara Stanbridge wrote in an IHM history. Sister Theresa, in what's been described as self-imposed exile, left Pennsylvania to join the Sisters of Charity of Ottawa, Ontario. In this photograph, she wears the habit of the "Grey Nuns" of Ottawa. In 1885, she was allowed to rejoin the Immaculata IHM congregation near Philadelphia. She died there at age 81 on January 4, 1892. The three IHM congregations are independent of each other, with different governing constitutions and some different priorities in ministry. They unite for meetings every five years and will meet in Monroe in 2020 along with the Oblate Sisters of Providence from Baltimore, where Sister Theresa first entered religious life.

This building served as the IHM Motherhouse from 1866 to 1932. A statue of Mary, the order's patroness, was perched above the entrance.

This photograph, believed to date to the 1880s, gives a view of the IHM campus on the north bank of the River Raisin. The buildings included St. Mary Academy, a convent, and an orphanage the sisters operated from 1855 to 1895.

Motherhouse, 1866-1932, main entrance

Here is a postcard of the St. Mary Academy that was built in 1904, after the school had outgrown a facility built in 1881. It was adjacent to St. Mary Church in Monroe. The school enrolled more than 300 girls, and students came from New York, Nevada, and Montana to be educated at the boarding school. Beginning in 1905, the school started offering college classes, and it became known as St. Mary College and Academy.

This is the transom, made in 1869, that hung over an entrance at the IHM Motherhouse and, later, St. Mary Academy. Decades after the buildings were demolished, the transom ended up in a Texas antique store. The IHMs reacquired it for $132.09, including shipping. It is on display at the Motherhouse Archives Heritage Display. At left is a statue of Mary that dates back to the 1880s. (Photograph by Patricia Montemurri.)

On June 4, 2010, Pres. William Howard Taft visited Monroe and addressed St. Mary Academy students. The *Detroit Free Press* proclaimed: "President's Heart Is Touched by Reception of St. Mary's: In Lovely Gowns of White, 250 Young Girls Greet Distinguished Guest with Simple Ceremony that Leaves Deep Impress on Him." Taft was in Monroe for the unveiling of a statue commemorating Gen. George Armstrong Custer, who considered Monroe his hometown after moving to the city in his teens and marrying a local. Custer died during his ill-fated command of the Battle of the Little Bighorn on June 25, 1876. (Above, courtesy of Walter P. Reuther Library, Wayne State University.)

When automotive pioneer Henry Ford and his wife, Clara, celebrated their 40th wedding anniversary, they were feted at an April 11, 1929, reception at St. Mary Academy (above). Students staged a folk dance festival (below) as part of the evening's entertainment. Henry Ford, raised Episcopalian, knew about the IHMs thanks to the family of Sr. Miriam Raymo. As a young entrepreneur operating a bicycle shop, Ford frequented a Detroit hardware store owned by the Raymo family. Every year, Ford would donate a car to the IHMs. On August 17, 1939, Ford's secretary, Ernest G. Liebold, delivered the five-millionth V-8 model Ford to Monroe as a special gift.

Fire destroyed St. Mary Academy in June 1929 (above). No one was hurt. Below, St. Mary Academy students gather in 1931 for the ground-breaking ceremony for their new school. Replacing St. Mary Academy was a formidable challenge. The congregation of 737 sisters borrowed $3.5 million in 1931. When the debt was paid off in 1976, the IHM congregation numbered 1,174.

Under IHM Monroe general superior Mother Ruth Hankerd, the IHMs constructed the landmark Monroe IHM campus. The above photograph shows the new St. Mary Academy under construction. The new building opened in 1932 with an enrollment of 340 girls in 12 grades. Architect August C. Bohlen & Son designed the campus. The *Monroe Evening News* described it as a "collection of masterpieces" and "a remarkable achievement in finance, planning and construction." The center is marked by an 11-ton statue of Mary carved from Italian Carrara marble. (Above, courtesy of Walter P. Reuther Library, Wayne State University.)

Two

TAKING THE VEIL

From 1894 to 1938, Mother Leocadia Delanty was the IHM Monroe mistress of novices—women mostly in their late teens and in the second year of convent life and training. They remained novices for about two years before taking their final vows and becoming "professed" sisters. In this August 15, 1931, photograph, Mother Leocadia sits with her novices, who wear white veils to distinguish themselves from the professed sisters, who wear black veils over royal blue habits. Traditionally, nuns and sisters wore habits as an outward sign of commitment to religious life. Habits derive from the common dress of the European Middle Ages. The veil symbolized a shield from the outside community, and accents of a white collar or white wimple over the chest signified purity. The black veil worn by Mother Leocadia symbolized the full repudiation of the outside world. Those rigid rules changed after the Second Vatican Council, a rare summit first convened under Pope John XXIII from 1962 to 1965. The Roman Catholic Church gave greater roles to the laity and choice to religious orders. But for about 121 years, until 1966, IHM professed sisters were required to don the full habit.

It was common for women to enter the convent in their late teen years. In her first year, she was called a postulant, from the word *postulate*, for she asked to be received into the congregation to explore whether religious life was right for her. Today, they are called candidates. In these 1945 photographs, postulants play table tennis and softball during the daily recreation period while wearing black net caps, black dresses, and short capes with white collars.

These pictures belie the rules that enforced silence for much of an IHM postulant's day. In the above photo, postulants enjoy a roller-skating break. Below, Sister Alphonsus Mary Charboneau leads a St. Patrick's Day–themed sing-along. Sister Joan (Marie Trinite) Glisky wrote in *Building Sisterhood* that an IHM spent two-thirds of her day in silence. "Conversation with one another was allowed only at recreation times. The afternoon was marked as a time of stricter silence to honor Jesus' agony on the cross. After school chatting was unknown. From 8:30 p.m. until after meditation in the morning, a 'solemn silence' was to be observed—a time that did not permit even a whisper (or a glance) except in emergency." Even during recreation times, conversation was limited to certain places and prohibited in the dormitory, corridors, or even on the street.

Here are some IHM regulations for 1950s-era IHM postulants, who are studying in silence in this photograph, as recounted in a 2016 issue of *IHM Archives Notes*. About letter writing: "Postulants receive mail about once a month. Your daughter will write to you on the Sunday nearest the 25th, and will receive your answer to her letter around the first of each month. Ordinarily mail will not be distributed in between times, although if there is anything urgent you may be sure a note to your daughter will receive consideration." Immediate family members—parents, grandparents, and siblings—could visit from "two to five o'clock" on eight specified days between September and June, and when visiting, parents weren't allowed to bring food or treats to share with their daughters. "Since the postulant must take her meals in the refectory with the other sisters, and may not eat anything outside of meal time without permission, please do not expect her to partake of anything with you when you visit her."

After a period ranging from nine months to one year, an IHM postulant became a novice. She wore a full-length blue serge habit with a white veil to distinguish her from the professed or vowed sisters, who wore black veils. There was a wake-up bell at 5:00 a.m., as shown in the photograph at right, and bells until the 9:30 p.m. bedtime. No chitchat was allowed during meals (below) except on Saturdays and Sunday afternoons.

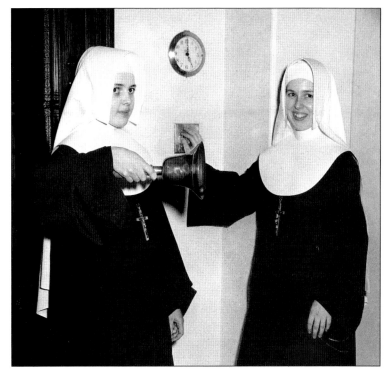

Postulants were only allowed to speak to other postulants during approved times. Novices were only allowed to speak to other novices and not to the postulants below them or the older professed sisters unless they were sharing a class, as in the above photograph. The novices had their own choir, pictured below. Regardless of rank, IHMs could talk freely on the Sunday closest to the 25th of each month at "Infant's Circle" gatherings—a name associated with Jesus's arrival on December 25th. Chocolates and sweets were the day's treat.

There was a grand ceremony when a postulant became an IHM novice. She started the day wearing "bridal white" and would end the day veiled in a nun's habit. During the reception into the congregation, IHM postulants wore identical white satin gowns. In earlier years, IHMs actually wore bridal gowns. The white gown was a symbol of a sister pledging her life to the Lord, as a bride takes a groom. The above photograph features some of the 1946 reception participants. In the 1953 photograph at right, family and friends fill the Motherhouse chapel for the ceremony.

At the 1946 reception, postulants kneel in front of the chapel altar in their white satin gowns. Later in the ceremony, the postulants return to the altar wearing the full-length habit and white veil of a novice IHM, as do the novice sisters (to the right in the above image). Below, the postulants lie prostrate on the cold marble floor in front of the altar to demonstrate meekness and humility in becoming a servant of God.

The postulants above carry their new habits for the June 1962 reception ceremony. After retreating to a private room, they would again flow into the Motherhouse chapel changed into full-length blue IHM habits, their waists cinched by a wooden rosary, a cross displayed on their white wimples, and their heads draped in the novice's white veil. Below, new IHM novices gather, with some adjusting the fit of their veils.

When she became a novice, an IHM was given a new name to signify a separate identity in religious life. She could make three suggestions, but her superiors made the pick. Sometimes, a woman suggested the name of a parent or a favorite Catholic saint. On rare occasions, superiors gave the sister her own name. Above, a priest announces a novice's religious name in the 1963 ceremony.

After two years as a novice, an IHM made her first vows to receive her black veil. After several more years, she made her perpetual, or final, vows. She received a ring—a thin gold band symbolic of her dedication to Christ. In the above photograph, sisters emerge from the service at which they received their black veils.

Three

MOTHERHOUSE MEMORIES

The IHMs
operated St.
Mary Farm from
1920 to 1976. It
covered 1,100
acres of farmland
split between the
Motherhouse
and plots about
six miles away.
The IHMs raised
crops, poultry,
sheep, and dairy
and beef cattle
and tended to the
fruit orchards.
Farm work was
not unknown to
many IHMs, who
grew up on farms
in Michigan and
the Midwest. The
sisters worked
in their habits,
plus an apron.

In these 1945 photographs, IHM Sisters pose after a harvest (above), and novice IHMs, wearing white veils, pick berries (at left). The IHMs hired farmhands for a great deal of the work, but during World War II, there were not enough men around for them to employ. Sisters took on more duties in the field, especially during summer breaks from their teaching assignments. (Below, courtesy of Walter P. Reuther Library, Wayne State University.)

St. Mary Farm produced enough milk, meat, produce, and fruit to satisfy the needs of the Motherhouse and St. Mary Academy. Often, there was enough to send to many other parish convents around Detroit where IHM Sisters lived while teaching in Catholic schools. Above, a trio of IHMs, including Sister Cyrilla (Marion) Farrell (center), tend to the sheep. At right, a sister checks out egg production. At Thanksgiving, turkeys from St. Mary Farm were distributed to IHM convents.

To get to the farm, IHM Sisters had use of a jeep. Below, IHM Sisters have a canning bee to preserve orchard pears. From about the 1930s through the 1950s, the IHMs dispatched driver John Jackson each week to bring food to IHM-staffed convents.

Who knew that life as a Catholic sister would involve the use of a mangle? It was in the IHM Motherhouse laundry and used to iron bedding and other household items.

Sisters who tended to the Motherhouse's infirmary unit wore white habits and veils. While most IHMs were teachers, several studied for nursing degrees to care for aging members. The five-story Liguori Hall was added to the back of the Motherhouse in 1962 to care for infirm sisters.

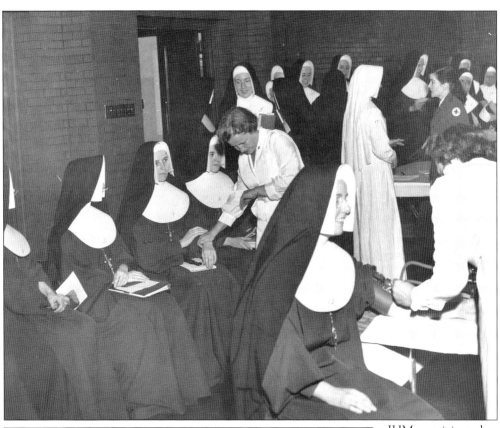

IHMs participated in a 1956 blood drive sponsored by the Monroe County Red Cross. In a similar 1958 event, some 96 IHMs each gave a pint of blood, which led the field of organizations participating to help the local Red Cross blood bank.

The IHMs sought to provide for their sisters' most basic needs. That included shoes, black with sensible soles, that were stacked high and wide in the Motherhouse shoe room.

In 1878, Eleanor Sibbald was the 147th woman to enter the IHM congregation. As Sister Germaine, she taught herself how to paint. She had a studio and sketching porch on the top floor of St. Mary Academy. Before she died in 1955, she painted numerous portraits of IHM superiors, including Mother Mary Joseph Walker, IHM superior from 1859 to 1864.

In 1945, the Sisters, Servants of the Immaculate Heart of Mary marked their centennial. Cofounder Sr. Theresa Maxis Duchemin established the Monroe IHMs in 1845 and founded two IHM congregations in Pennsylvania. Sisters from all three branches gathered in Monroe to celebrate. These IHM dolls were on display. The IHMs' original habit was black. In 1847, the habit remained black but with an overlay of blue fabric (known as the scapular). By 1854, the entire habit was blue.

Some 140 families have watched two or more siblings become IHMs. Of those, 13 families gave three daughters to the IHM Motherhouse. The Sullivan family sent five daughters to Monroe between 1932 and 1943. They are, from left to right in the first row, Srs. Genevieve (Mary Clifford), Angela, Margaret (Malachy), Marie Sylvia, and Janet. In 2019, Sister Janet celebrated her 75th year as an IHM, and Sister Genevieve marked her 77th year. Sister Margaret died at age 101 in 2018, Sister Angela died in 2004, and Sister Marie Sylvia died in 1994.

Three daughters of US representative Louis Rabaut (third from right) entered the IHMs. From left to right are Srs. Celeste (Palmyra) and Stella Rabaut; their mother, Stella; their father; Sr. Martha Marie Rabaut; and their brother, Jesuit priest Rev. Dermott Rabaut. Congressman Rabaut was credited with introducing legislation to insert "under God" into the Pledge of Allegiance. (Courtesy of Gesu Parish; photograph by Nemo Warr.)

It was headline news when two IHM Sisters took flight. On May 27, 1948, Mother Teresa McGivney (right) and Sister Mary McGrath (left), pictured boarding the plane, became the first IHMs to fly on a plane. St. Mary Academy and Marygrove College alumnae gave the sisters a European vacation. At Willow Run Airport, near Ypsilanti, a crowd of well-wishers (above) gathered on the tarmac before the IHMs flight to New York. From New York, the IHMs sailed to Southampton, England. Their European tour also included a 20-minute audience with Pope Pius XII in Rome before they took a transatlantic flight home.

Mother Anna Marie Grix was the IHM general superior from 1954 to 1966 and was lauded for her skilled leadership of the congregation at its peak. Outside of southeastern Michigan, she opened schools in California, Missouri, Illinois, Florida, and Alabama. Pictured here are, from left to right, Mother Grix, Mother Teresa McGivney, Mother Ruth Hankerd, and Sisters Miriam Raymo and Francis Regis Kelly.

With suitcases in hand, sisters leave the Motherhouse for teaching assignments, known as missions. Under Mother Anna Marie Grix, hundreds of IHMs spent their summers studying in graduate programs at Catholic colleges and state universities.

Four

BREAKING GROUND IN EDUCATION

Detroit was booming in 1922, when the IHMs paid $241,000 for land on the city's northern edge to build Marygrove College. Mother Domitilla Donahue broke ground in 1925. The congregation borrowed $4 million—the equivalent of nearly $58 million today—to erect and equip the college. It opened in September 1927 with 287 students. Because of rising costs, declining enrollment, and dwindling forecasts for college-age students, the Marygrove Trustees and the IHM Leadership Council closed Marygrove in December 2019. Under a nonprofit initiative called the Marygrove Conservancy, the Kresge Foundation is committed to preserving the 53-acre campus and pioneering new education initiatives. The campus is slated to become a P-20 (preschool to community college) facility for the Detroit Public Schools Community District and a teaching laboratory for the University of Michigan. Marygrove's Sacred Heart Chapel will remain open.

This aerial photograph offers a glimpse of the early Marygrove campus located at West McNichols Road (Six Mile) and Wyoming Avenue in northwest Detroit. The first buildings were the Liberal Arts Building, pictured at center and home to the Sacred Heart Chapel, and Madame Cadillac Hall, the long building nestled among the trees, which was the women's dormitory. (Courtesy of Walter P. Reuther Library, Wayne State University.)

IHMs encircle workmen placing a statue of the Blessed Mother Mary on the Marygrove College campus in September 1927. The 9-foot marble statue, which sits atop a 50-foot column, was later named *Our Lady of Marygrove*. The college's first president was George Hermann Derry, the first layperson to helm a US Catholic women's college. The 1930 commencement speaker, Fr. Henry Smith, president of the Catholic University of America, declared that Marygrove "is an object of envy to all Catholic institutions in the land."

Catholic sisters representing a variety of congregations in the Detroit area are shown touring Marygrove College. The Marygrove records cite several occasions when sisters from other congregations visited. (Courtesy of Walter P. Reuther Library, Wayne State University.)

As an all-girls Catholic college, Marygrove had strict rules concerning male visitors and curfews. The gates to the college entrance were closed at night. In this undated photograph, a suitor chats with a Marygrove student on the steps outside Madame Cadillac Hall.

Marygrove College has conferred thousands of degrees in its 92-year history. In the above photograph, Catherine O'Neill (placing a lily) and Josephine Irving (behind O'Neill) became two of them in 1940, when Detroit archbishop Edward Mooney conferred degrees on 69 seniors. In the 1960s photograph at left, three graduates are exuberant about finishing college.

Toting laundry bags and suitcases, a few IHM Sisters at Marygrove moved into a new campus convent on September 12, 1949. Their previous quarters had been converted into student housing. From left to right are Sisters Ann Terese Linskey, Susanne Krupp, Clement Marie Zittel, Alphonsus Marie (Louise) Sawkins, and Mary Vianney Conrey.

Marygrove 1959 alumna Barbara Lemhagen is striding the runway for a 1961 tea and fashion show fundraiser. The student-run newspaper *Campus Reporter* noted that $12,300 was raised for scholarships—equivalent to $100,000 today.

Above, Marygrove students help librarian Sr. Claudia Carlen move books into an enlarged library. As part of a good-natured freshman initiation at Marygrove College in 1968, first-year students wore beanies, nicknamed "dinks." In the c. 1968 picture at left, taken in Marygrove's Library Lecture Hall, student Patsy Reilly Peters (far left in the front row) wears a beanie while taking notes for a world culture class. Seated next to her is Janice Noonan Percheron. Behind them, in beanies, are Cathy Haven (left) and Renée Ahee.

In 1963, sisters from a variety of Catholic congregations gather for a photography workshop at Marygrove organized by *Detroit Free Press* photographer Bert Emmanuele.

Marygrove's roots date to 1910, when it began as St. Mary's College in Monroe. It was renamed and relocated to Detroit in 1927. Thus, in 1960, it was time to celebrate the college's 50th anniversary. Marking the occasion are, clockwise from far left at the table, IHM Srs. Marie Fidelis Remski, Frances Gabriel Hess, Kevin Marie (Ann) Hannon, Marie Ellen Clanon, Trinita Schilling, Marie Constance Hackett, Loretta Mary Tenbusch, and Venard Murphy. In the foreground are Srs. Stanislaus (Mary Anne) Huddleston (left) and Ann Joseph Fix.

Sr. Mary Emil Penet, Marygrove's president from 1961 to 1968, had a vision that shaped Catholic education across the country. She helped develop the Sister Formation Conference in the 1950s, which was designed to ensure that Catholic sisters received college educations before becoming classroom teachers and be allowed to pursue graduate degrees in their specialties. This peeved Catholic bishops, who relied on the sisters to staff Catholic schools for little money. The Sister Formation movement meant that Catholic schools had to hire more lay teachers, who received higher pay than sisters. For example, the Archdiocese of Detroit paid only $40 a month to a teaching sister. That went up to $70 in 1956, according to IHM records. Without the savings generated by the pittances paid to teaching sisters, according to the March 2011 *IHM Archives Notes*, "it is doubtful that the system of Catholic schools, unparalleled in other countries, would have flourished as it did." Sister Mary Emil's advocacy was not popular among Catholic bishops, but the sisters persisted. When she addressed the 1952 National Catholic Education Association Convention about the issue, "the sisters in attendance gave her a standing ovation: the superintendents were upset and stayed in their seats." As Marygrove president, she also lobbied the Michigan legislature to pass the Michigan Tuition Grant Program in 1966. It continues to help students in need with up to $2,400 in grants to attend a private or public nonprofit college or university.

In 1971, Marygrove College opened to male students. "Marygrove Coed? Sure Is. Get With It, Men," proclaimed an ad. Marygrove was not immune to Detroit's economic and racial struggles. Under Sr. Mary Emil Penet's presidency, Marygrove joined the neighborhood organization the Fitzgerald Community Council in supporting integration. "The acid test of our sincerity in banding together in this Community Council is whether in our heart of hearts we ever would want a lily-white neighborhood here if we could have it," Sister Mary Emil said at a press conference. "We would not want it." Her successor, Sr. Jane Mary Howard, initiated "68 for '68" to recruit more African American students (the first black student had enrolled in 1938). The program offered scholarships to top students from Detroit public and Catholic high schools. By 1969, one-quarter of the incoming 260-member class was African American.

These graduates are among the last of some 44,000 alumni who have earned undergraduate and graduate degrees from Marygrove College, opened by the IHMs in 1927. They received graduate degrees in a commencement ceremony on May 10, 2019, at the Detroit landmark. Marygrove College closed on December 31, 2019, because of declining enrollment and deep debt. Those factors have caused the closing or consolidation of more than 20 small US liberal arts colleges between 2016 and 2019. The IHMs have created the Marygrove Conservancy under the stewardship of the Kresge Foundation, which is funding Marygrove's transformation into a "cradle-to-career" campus—for preschool to community college education—with the Detroit Public Schools Community District, the University of Michigan, and Starfish Family Services. "Marygrove College has been filling a unique and vital niche in higher education in Detroit since we opened the doors in 1927," said Marygrove president Elizabeth Burns on June 12, 2019. "Those of us who love Marygrove will be helped in coming to grips with this decision knowing that the Sisters' mission of education will continue on in this special place. This is indeed an incredibly sad and heartbreaking day for everyone: Marygrove, higher education, our alumni, students, faculty, staff, our neighbors, and the city of Detroit. But the spirit of those who came before will imbue the Marygrove values in those who come after." She later added in an interview in the summer 2019 edition of the *Marygrove Tower Times*: "The memories of generations of students, the lessons taught and learned, and the friendships made and cherished will live on, all kept sacred by Our Lady of Marygrove."

Five

CLASSROOM LESSONS

The Sisters, Servants of the Immaculate Heart of Mary were the area's predominant teaching congregation in the classrooms at Catholic schools in southeastern Michigan in the mid-1900s. At Our Lady of Mount Carmel in Emmett, Sister Kathleen Mary O'Brien taught 49 first- and second-graders in one classroom of the four-room school in 1958–1959. The IHMs operated the school from 1924 until its closing in 1971. The arc of Sister Kate's service illustrates how IHMs found new ministries as many Catholic schools closed after the Baby Boomer generation passed through the pipeline. She broke ground as the first female chaplain to work in the Texas prison system at a women's correctional facility in Gatesville. She is an award-winning painter and also has worked as a hospice chaplain. But for many of the estimated 700,000 students taught by IHMs, this image illustrates how the women are remembered. They may not be in the traditional classroom anymore, but they continue to show the depth and impact of their faith.

UNIVERSITY OF MICHIGAN
IDENTIFICATION CARD
1932-1933
(Good for current college year only)

Sister M. Ambrosia I.H.M

SIGNATURE IN FULL

517 Elizabeth   *9614*

ANN ARBOR ADDRESS   TEL. NO.

St. Mary Consent Monroe Mich.

HOME ADDRESS

is enrolled as a student in the University of Michigan.

Joseph W. Bursley.

No. _____   DEAN OF STUDENTS

SISTER M
AMBROSIA I.HM

Sister Ambrosia Fitzgerald was one of the first women to earn a doctorate in physics from the University of Michigan. This was her student identification card for the 1932–1933 school year. While attending UM, she lived at St. Thomas the Apostle Parish. She taught at Marygrove College, St. Mary Academy, Detroit St. Mary of Redford, St. Gregory, Immaculata, and Holy Redeemer High Schools. During World War II, she secretly travelled to Chicago to work on the Manhattan Project, which led to the development of the atomic bomb.

Just west of the current IHM Motherhouse sits the original Hall of the Divine Child, a school sponsored and built by the IHMs in 1918. It was a military-style boarding school for boys, and the band played on. Among its youthful boarders was US representative John D. Dingell Jr., whose tenure from 1955 to 2015, representing the Detroit area, marked the longest in Congressional history. Hall of the Divine Child closed in 1980. It is now a 109-unit senior residence, Norman Towers.

Hall of the Divine Child principal Sr. Theotilda (Alice) O'Hara greets her charges in this 1960 photograph. In the summer, IHMs returning to the Motherhouse campus from school assignments also lived here. This is where Sister Theotilda caught some young IHMs sunbathing on an upper back porch, their veils pushed aside, their shoes and stockings doffed, their habits pulled up around them. Their punishment was having their Saturday talking privileges revoked.

IHMs taught at Most Holy Trinity Catholic School in Detroit from 1867 until the 2000s—among the longest stretches of IHM ministry at one parish school. Good workers they were, as this sign proclaims above three IHMs, including former IHM Sr. Ruth Ann Nauer (left), Sr. Regina Fanning (center) and Sr. Juanita Bernard. Holy Trinity School remained open for the 2019–2020 school year, one of only four Catholic grade schools still open in Detroit.

Servants of the Imn

May God's Providence continue to bless Holy Redee

Bottom Row, left to right: Sisters Jane Frances, Marie Christine, Boniface
Ida Therese, Alicia, Vita Marie. 2nd Row: Sisters Aloyse, Irene, Lellis, M
Anacletus. 3rd Row: Sisters Mary Lawrence, Herman Joseph, Mauraleen,
Reginald, Edwardine, Laurena, Eucharia, Ann Bernardette, Patrick Ellen,
Liseaux, Clare Elizabeth, Frances Jerome, Paracleta, Marie Madeline,

Holy Redeemer Catholic Parish, on Detroit's southwest side, was one of the nation's largest parishes in the mid-1900s. There were 14 Masses on Sundays to accommodate the crowds. In 1945, the parish elementary school had 1,401 students, while the high school enrolled 730, according to *Achievement of a Century*, a book prepared for the IHM centennial by Sr. M. Rosalita Kelly. She recorded that there were 48 sisters assigned to Holy Redeemer schools in 1945, aided by one lay teacher. There were 54 IHMs living in the Holy Redeemer convent when this photograph was taken. Holy Redeemer Elementary School opened in 1882 and continued into its 136th year of operation in 2019–2020. Holy Redeemer High School closed in 2005, but IHMs cosponsored the creation of a new high school in the building. Detroit Cristo Rey High School opened in 2008, and students work at a variety of jobs one day per week to help pay for tuition. The Holy Redeemer convent closed in 2004 and was later demolished. IHM Sisters were not the only people

Rita, Joavan, Mother Mary Patrick, John Mary, Joanella, Margaret Marie,
, Mary Lambert, Althea, Regis Mary, Rebecca, Loretta Cecile, Stephane,
Rose Bernadette, Ann Leo, Marie Julia, Muriel. 4th Row: Sisters Mary
, Patrice, Dolorosa. Top Row: Sisters Ignatius, Frederick Marie, Therese
Marie Clotilde.

who lived there. Actor Donald Sutherland boarded at the convent in 1986 while filming *The Rosary Murders*, in which he played a fictional crime-solving priest. In the convent kitchen, he played a short-order cook, whipping up breakfast pancakes for 13 IHM Sisters. More than 100 women from Holy Redeemer Parish became IHM Sisters. By 1961, there were 539 IHM Sisters teaching at Catholic schools within the city of Detroit, including Blessed Sacrament, All Saints, Annunciation, Epiphany, Girls Catholic Central, Immaculata, Our Lady of Good Counsel, Our Lady of Help, Our Lady Queen of Hope, Mother of Our Savior, St. Agnes, St. Boniface, St. Catherine of Siena, St. Cecilia, St. Charles Borromeo, St. Francis de Sales, St. George, St. Gregory, St. Joseph, St. Martin, St. Mary of Redford, St. Matthew, St. Patrick, St. Rose of Lima, St. Thomas Aquinas, and St. Vincent.

IHM Sisters accompany students dressed in their First Communion finery at Christ the King Elementary School in Detroit. The school is one of four Catholic elementary schools still open in Detroit in 2019–2020. Compare that to the 108 Catholic elementary schools in Detroit and the enclaves of Hamtramck and Highland Park in the mid-1960s.

In 1925, the IHMs inaugurated Detroit Gesu Catholic School. Here, an IHM oversees Girl Scouts in position for a May crowning procession in 1961. One of the four remaining Catholic grade schools in Detroit, Gesu enrolled more than 250 students for the 2019–2020 school year. In 2015, the IHMs initiated a campaign to digitize alumni records of the four grade schools, all of which were once staffed by IHMs, to help the schools with fundraising.

The IHM congregation built the all-girls Immaculata High School in 1941 along the eastern edge of the Marygrove College campus. Immaculata High, along with Hall of the Divine Child, St. Mary Academy, and Marygrove College, were considered "sponsored" institutions, meaning that the IHM congregation financed and staffed the schools. In other instances, the Detroit archdiocese or parish priests asked the IHMs to teach in schools. Above is the Immaculata crest. Immaculata opened on September 8, 1941, with 94 seniors (pictured below), 121 juniors, 154 sophomores, and 160 freshmen.

Several sisters involved in teaching French ham it up at Immaculata. They include Srs. Antoinette Ruedisueli (center) and Chrysostom Truka (second from right). Both IHMs taught at nearby Marygrove College from 1962 to 1964. When Sister Antoinette died in August 2009 at age 84, she was the first IHM to request a "green burial," eschewing traditional practices and opting for a biodegradable casket in the west corner of the IHMs' St. Mary Cemetery.

Some 7,000 young women graduated from Immaculata. Because of a decline in enrollment, Immaculata closed in 1983. Here is a photograph of students outside the school in 1978. Since then, the building has been reused as a Detroit Public Schools magnet academy and as a charter school; it has also stood empty. The building is scheduled to see new life in the 2021–2022 school year as a public elementary school as part of the reuse of the Marygrove College campus.

Parents from five parishes—Birmingham Holy Name and St. Columban, Southfield St. Bede, Beverly Hills Our Lady Queen of Martyrs, and Bloomfield Hills St. Hugo of the Hills—asked the IHMs to build and staff an all-girls high school north of Detroit. The parent committee raised about $1 million, and IHMs remortgaged the Monroe Motherhouse to pay for the rest. Ground was broken in 1959, and the cornerstone ceremony is depicted in this image. Marian High School opened later that year with a ninth-grade class of 132 girls.

In 1987, Marian High added a science wing. Srs. Lorraine (Paul Joseph) Humphrey (center) and Helen (Marianna) Glaser (to the right of Sister Lorraine) watch as principal Sr. Joan (Joseph Andre) Charnley digs in.

Sr. Mary Aquin (Anne) Chester was principal of Marian High School from 1960 to 1966. A labyrinth on the Motherhouse campus is dedicated in her memory.

Marian High continues to thrive. It has distinguished itself in academics, and the Marian Mustangs have won 27 state athletic championships between 1988 and 2018 in basketball, soccer, tennis, swimming and diving, skiing, figure skating, volleyball, and lacrosse. Photographed outside Marian's main entrance in March 2019 are students (from left to right) Izabel Toma, Adriana Kalabat, Makayla Snyder, and Kathryn Corden. (Photograph by Rachel Smith.)

The first IHM-sponsored school was St. Mary Academy, opened in 1846 by the congregation's first members. In this photograph, biology teacher Sr. Veronica Mary Maher gathers with St. Mary Academy girls on the school grounds. She earned advanced degrees in molecular biology and taught for 30 years at Michigan State University's medical school, was a cofounder of its Carcinogenesis Laboratory, and was an associate dean of graduate study. She was awarded Michigan State's highest honor, the title of university distinguished professor. She died in 2017.

Valerie Harper (right), the late actress who played Jewish TV sitcom character Rhoda Morgenstern, boarded at St. Mary Academy in 1949 for fifth grade. She visited the IHM Motherhouse in 2013 and met with her IHM teachers, including Sr. Frances Gabriel Hess. St. Mary Academy closed in 1988 and merged with the all-boys Monroe Catholic Central. The resulting coed school operates at the former boys' school site, which is on land previously occupied by the St. Mary Academy school building that was destroyed in a 1929 fire.

The Monroe IHMs opened the all-girls Immaculate Heart of Mary High School in Westchester, outside of Chicago, in 1961. In the above photograph, students move into the school after they initially attended classes in a wing of the neighboring boys' school because of construction delays. At its peak, the high school enrolled some 1,400 girls, and 42 sisters worked there. The mid-1960s faculty is pictured below. Some 6,000 women graduated from Immaculate Heart of Mary High School before it closed in 2005.

Our Lady of Help Catholic School operated just east of Detroit's downtown. The IHMs staffed the school beginning in 1875. It bordered the city's African American neighborhood, historically known as Black Bottom because of its rich soil, as well as streets filled with working-class European immigrants. This image features an IHM Sister and her charges. The area—along with the parish—was bulldozed for mid-1960s urban renewal developments.

Holy Name School, founded in 1928 in the Detroit suburb of Birmingham, opened for its 91st school year in 2019. In this 1964 photograph, hands are raised to answer Sr. William Mary (Carolyn) Campbell's question. She has worked as a principal at Academia Santa Teresita in Santurce, Puerto Rico; St. Michael in Miami; and St. Albert the Great in Dearborn Heights. She also has ministered as a hospital chaplain at ProMedica Regional Hospital in Monroe.

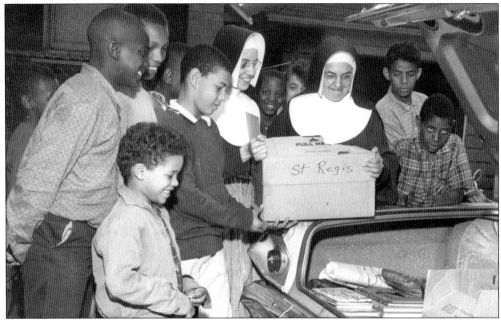

St. George Catholic School closed in 1965 and was eventually bulldozed to make way for the Interstate 75 Chrysler Freeway on Detroit's east side. For many years, its students were the children of Lithuanian immigrants. IHM Sisters served there when the school enrolled many African Americans. Srs. Louise (Rose Mary) Ala (left) and Mary Alan (Catherine) Cavataio are handling a load of religious books in this 1964 photograph. One of the first Detroit schools staffed by IHMs was called St. Augustine, established by the pastor of the historic Ste. Anne de Detroit Parish to provide schooling for black children. It operated for just three years—from 1867 to 1870.

This schoolboy at St. John the Baptist in Monroe gets help with his galoshes from Sr. Jannita Marie Complo. As an education doctoral student, she developed a curriculum, Dramakinetics, that uses movement and drama to help children learn. She used it in nationally honored work with the Jemez Indians in New Mexico. For 19 years in Monroe, she ran the Children's Creativity Center to help children with special needs.

Not many IHMs knew how to drive, let alone had access to a car. Sisters relied on volunteer drivers while they were missioned out to parishes. Flint-area Ford dealer Thomas Sullivan (far left) donated a green Ford sedan to the IHMs staffing St. John School in Fenton on November 21, 1954. Rev. John Madden blessed the car for, from left to right, Srs. Carol (Jean) Hengesbaugh (who had a driver's license); Francine Malzone; Cyprian Maurer, principal; and Bernetta Booms.

IHMs staffed St. Philip School in Battle Creek beginning in 1884. Here, Sr. Inez (Rita) Dubois imparts a lesson to Girl and Boy Scouts at the school.

Sr. Adele DuRoss is pictured with students at Sacred Heart Elementary School in the Detroit suburb of Roseville, where she was principal from 1963 to 1965. During 40 years in education, she was a teacher or principal at a dozen schools.

In 1965, Our Lady of Good Counsel students brought holiday cheer to residents at St. Joseph's Home for the Aged on Detroit's east side. Sr. Faustina (Audrey) Crepeau (far left) taught an eighth-grade class of 47 students that year. Standing next to her is Sr. Mary Norman (Lucille) Finehart, who had 46 students in her sixth-grade class. The school closed in the early 1990s.

In this mid-1960s photograph, IHM Sisters look on at a party in the basement of St. Francis Xavier School in Otisville, about 24 miles north of Flint.

Sr. Ann Matthew Murie and students welcome visitors to St. Hugo of the Hills in the Detroit suburb of Bloomfield Hills around 1962. St. Hugo, which opened in 1940 with 4 IHMs and 50 students, recorded its 80th year of operation in 2019–2020. Years later, Sister Ann Matthew also taught at St. Edward's University in Austin, Texas. St. Edward's was an all-male college, and the IHMs had been asked to start a partner women's college, Maryhill, there in 1966. However, three years later, Maryhill was absorbed into a newly coed St. Edward's.

Sr. Jean Ann Healy is looking good and in charge of a school playground in this photograph. She taught for decades in Detroit-area schools, including Wyandotte St. Patrick, Detroit Holy Redeemer, and Wayne St. Mary, before retiring from St. Edith in Livonia. She died in 1997 at the age of 75.

IHMs arrived at St. Boniface parish in Detroit's Corktown neighborhood, home to thousands of Irish immigrants, in 1872. Sr. Maureen (Ann Philip) Daly (at left) and another sister are surrounded by books and smiling faces in this late 1960s image. St. Boniface Church, closed and then bulldozed for a parking lot, was a familiar site to many Detroit baseball fans because it was close to the old Tiger Stadium.

Sr. Josephine (Mary Dominic) Sferrella sets up a jump ball on a school playground. She was principal at St. Anne and St. Boniface grade schools and Holy Redeemer High School in Detroit and was dean of students at Marygrove College. For 21 years, she was the Archdiocese of Chicago's director of data and research. "I've had thousands of kids in the classroom throughout the years. And you never know who you've touched in a special way. It is both gratifying and humbling," she said before her death in 2017.

In this photograph from the late 1960s, IHM Sisters pose with children on their First Holy Communion day at St. Francis Xavier School in Vassar, north of Frankenmuth, Michigan. The school has closed, but the parish maintains ties with Monroe IHMs. In 2018, the parish sewing circle sent 36 girls' dresses to IHM Sisters in Puerto Rico who minister to a needy community.

Monroe IHMs taught in several states, including Florida, New Mexico, and Alabama. Sr. Brigid Mary Wade (kneeling at far right) helped tend to goats while teaching at Our Lady of Miracles in Gustine, California, from 1963 to 1965. The school had students who hailed from the Azores Islands. Heifer International provided goats for the students to raise and later ship to needy families in the Azores.

This photograph was taken in the years just before the Monroe IHMs confronted the immense changes brought on by the Second Vatican Council. Striding ahead with the towers of St. Mary Academy in the background are, from left to right, Srs. Marianna (Helen) Glaser, Stanislaus (Mary Anne) Huddleston, Eustasia (Mary Jane) Baumann, Leorita Huver, unidentified, and Anthonita (Rita) Bryden.

Six

FAITH IN CHANGE AND PRAYER

In 1966, some 62 women arrived at the Monroe Motherhouse to enter the convent. Among them was Nancy Sylvester, who is in the foreground and facing right in this 1967 photograph. Within the next two years, many of her classmates departed the IHMs. The Second Vatican Council, which ran from 1962 to 1965, had given more freedom to religious congregations. Debate swirled about whether sisters should hew to traditional rituals or adopt new looks and ministries. Many sisters, young and old, left the IHMs. Within the Motherhouse, there were heated debates about modifying the habit or doing away with it. Some sisters feared they'd lose the respect of their students without one. Nancy Sylvester, schooled by IHMs at Chicago's St. Felicitas School, had an affection for the traditional ways. She thought of leaving, too. At the time, Sr. Margaret (Benedicta) Brennan, a pioneering female theologian, was the Monroe IHM superior. Under Sister Margaret's gentle, transformational guidance, Sister Nancy stayed. Sister Nancy's work over the next 50 years was not what she originally envisioned as an IHM, but it illustrates the vision of IHM leaders in expanding the sisters' impact around the world and within the Catholic Church. Sister Nancy is an authority on Catholic social justice teaching. She has been executive director of NETWORK, the national social justice lobby founded by Catholic sisters, and president of the Leadership Conference of Women Religious (LCWR), which represents the elected leaders of most Catholic sisters in the United States. In 2002, she founded the Institute for Communal Contemplation and Dialogue, which provides resources for the transformation of consciousness.

Sr. Candyce (Lauren) Rekart, who is circled in this photograph, remembers the day this picture was taken. She entered the IHMs with these women in 1965 and professed vows with the other novices in June 1968 at a Mass with the theme "YES FOREVER." In the years after Vatican II, however, not all of these women went on to become or remain IHM Sisters. But for Sister Candyce, the theme has rung true. She was in the first IHM class in which many IHMs were sent to study at out-of-state colleges and beyond the IHM-run Marygrove College. At Loyola University in Chicago, she studied Spanish. A few years later, she was sent to IHM missions in Puerto Rico, where she taught students from a poor neighborhood. "Those were very significant years in the Church and in religious life after Vatican II. We definitely were in 'renewal.' Change was constant," recalls Sister Candyce. "We were looking at religious life in a newer way, being part of the people, standing up for social issues with others and experiencing ourselves as women religious with a voice." She also taught youngsters with cognitive disabilities in Puerto Rico public schools and became a clinical psychologist, counseling sexual abuse victims. Since 2016, she has assisted women considering joining the IHMs and also has counseled women in addiction recovery. "I face the challenges of . . . two very different ministries, one with women and children in the very down-to earth struggles of life" and "the other in our community as we face fewer women entering religious life today." Sister Candyce is deeply committed to religious life as it evolves in the future. "We do not know what that future will look like. We do know that as IHM Sisters and Associates, we are deeply engaged with others in our concerns for social justice and that we see the spirit of our community to be aligned with God through the Liberating Mission of Jesus."

Detroit auxiliary bishop Thomas Gumbleton celebrates a Mass at the Motherhouse chapel in June 1968. IHM novices wore modified white veils, while professed sisters wore modified black veils.

In 1972, IHMs gathered in Monroe for a Chapter of Affairs, during which sisters elected leaders and debated issues affecting the congregation. Participating in the offertory procession at a Motherhouse Mass were, from left to right, (first row) Srs. Marion (Jane Marie) Shea and Audrey (Vinciana) Bushell; (second row) Srs. Mary Katherine (Michael Andrew) Hamilton and Polly (Paul Andre) LeDuc.

At Dearborn's Sacred Heart High School, yearbook photographs illustrate the changes in IHM habits. When Sr. Mary Arthur Van Antwerp became principal in 1967, she donned the full habit. That changed in the next few years, as these photographs illustrate. She also became known by her birth name, Ellen. Many sisters chose to resume using their baptismal names after the Second Vatican Council reforms. A Sacred Heart alumnus, comedian and actor Thom Sharp, had a local hit in 1977 with his song "They Don't Make Nun Names (Like That No More)." (Courtesy of Dearborn Sacred Heart Parish.)

There were many IHMs who elected to continue wearing habits. There were various iterations of the IHMs' blue habit and black veil. In this photograph, Sr. Mary (Marie Lawrence) Bankert wears a proposed shorter habit. Sr. Sharon (Mary Austin) Defever has donned a modified long habit, doing away with the attention-grabbing white wimple.

Sr. Mary Frederick Galbraith was the principal of Our Lady of Lourdes High School and served on civic organizations in the Detroit suburb of River Rouge. When the mayor asked her to run for city council, she initially declined, but supporters urged her on. With permission from Detroit cardinal John Dearden, she ran and won a two-year term, becoming the first woman elected to the office.

Many prayers were offered for Sr. Catherine Frances Mallon, who died in 1970. After a breast cancer diagnosis, she allowed her tumors to be used in experiments. Doctors at the Michigan Cancer Foundation (now known as the Karmanos Cancer Center in Detroit) marveled at how her cancer cells multiplied exponentially. Her cell line became known as MCF-7 and was dubbed "immortal." It is the most-studied breast cancer cell line in the world and has led to breakthroughs in treatment.

Sr. Margaret (Benedicta) Brennan led the Monroe IHMs through tumultuous change. She was elected the congregation's superior from 1966 to 1976. She was one of the first women religious to earn a doctorate degree in theology and the first female theology professor at Regis College at the University of Toronto. She served as president of the Leadership Conference of Women Religious (LCWR), a national organization of Catholic sisters, in 1972, during a time of great division because of the changes brought about by the Second Vatican Council. Sister Margaret died on April 28, 2016, at the age of 92. In an article written for *National Catholic Reporter*, Syracuse University professor Margaret Susan Thompson lauded the IHM's legacy: "Margaret was an extraordinary woman—prophetic leader among Catholic women religious, pioneer theologian, mother of the House of Prayer movement, spiritual director, teacher, mentor, prolific scholar. Yet her rootedness was among her sisters in her beloved congregation of Monroe, Mich., Sisters, Servants of the Immaculate Heart of Mary. It was there that she lived, prayed, laughed and loved, and where she was most fully herself." Benedictine Sister Joan Chittister, a renowned theologian, author, and speaker, wrote: "The work and spirit she left behind her lives on in religious life from one end of the country to the other. . . . I can see her yet standing like an oak tree in the middle of a summer storm, unshaken by it all but attuned and moved by every wind."

In 1972, under Sr. Margaret Brennan's stewardship, the IHMs opened the Visitation House of Prayer in Monroe, a place to study spirituality based on the House of Prayer movement. Sister Margaret had come to know its proponents, Redemptorist priest Rev. Bernard Haring and Trappist monk Thomas Merton, a mystic and theologian. Here, she addresses a meeting at Visitation House during the 1970s.

After Sr. Margaret Brennan stepped down, Sr. Mary (Mary Bede) Kinney was elected the IHM general superior, serving from 1976 to 1982. Here, Sister Mary addresses the congregation during the leadership change.

In 1977, the Monroe IHMs began the Associates movement to foster ties between IHM Sisters and women who left the congregation. The first associate was Sharon Carolin (left), a former vowed IHM Sister. Men also can become IHM Associates, such as Chuck Van Vleet (right). Associates are laypeople who participate in a period of spiritual guidance with an IHM mentor and make a commitment to align themselves with the IHMs' life and ministry. (Photograph by Patricia Montemurri.)

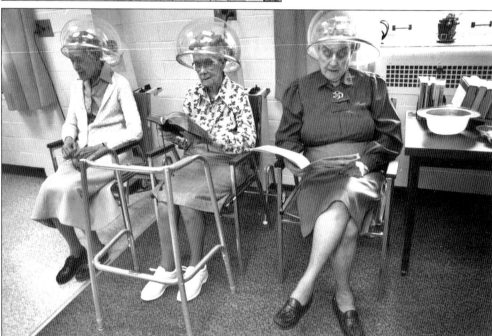

Everyday life changed at the Motherhouse in the late 20th century. It even got a hair salon. In this photograph, Sr. Teresina Gallagher (center) reads her prayer book during a 1993 appointment at the IHM hairdresser. (Courtesy of the *Detroit Free Press*; photograph by Pauline Lubens.)

While many IHMs stuck with the traditional habits, they also enjoyed new freedoms. In this 1980 photograph, Sr. Alma Reilly, 100 years old and an IHM for 73 of them, listens to a Detroit Tigers baseball game on the radio. That was a pleasure unavailable for her first decades as an IHM. The devotion to prayer remained a constant, however. The close-up at right shows how Sister Alma recited the rosary daily. (Both, courtesy of the *Detroit Free Press*; photograph by Patricia Beck.)

This photograph of IHMs attending Mass at Sacred Heart Catholic Church in Dearborn in 1979 shows how their clothing choices varied. This was a reunion for teachers who visited to celebrate the 50th anniversary of the church building. Sacred Heart High School closed in 1975. Its grade school has been open since 1918. (Courtesy of Dearborn Sacred Heart Parish.)

IHM Sister Claudia Carlen was a noted librarian, archivist, writer, and editor. Her renowned work on the writings of Catholic popes—known as encyclicals—gave her a unique perspective on the Church's evolution. Her five-volume *Papal Encyclicals 1740–1981* was the first comprehensive collection ever published.

In 1992, there was a gathering of Monroe IHMs as well as IHM Sisters from the Pennsylvania congregations based in Scranton and near Philadelphia (Immaculata). The three IHM congregations trace their inception to congregation cofounder Sr. Theresa Maxis Duchemin. On the agenda was a discussion of banding together to explore a feminist examination of IHM history. The Monroe and Scranton congregations backed the project, while the Philadelphia congregation declined. At left is then–IHM Monroe president Sr. Dorothy (Harold Marie) McDaniel.

Several Monroe IHM Sisters collaborated on *Building Sisterhood: A Feminist History of the Sisters, Servants of the Immaculate Heart of Mary*, published by Syracuse University Press in 1997. Among the contributors was Sr. Joan (Marie Trinite) Glisky, pictured with a copy of the book. In 1986, the Monroe IHM Constitutions were changed to state that sisters "consciously choose to educate ourselves to the feminist perspective." (Photograph by Patricia Montemurri.)

Sr. Ellen Clanon contributed to the essays in *Building Sisterhood*. In a 1993 *Detroit Free Press* article, the 87-year-old IHM called herself a "committed feminist." She explained: "It's not radical. It's the truth of what we're discovering about ourselves and appreciating." Many IHM predecessors were at the forefront of the feminist movement, she said, although they didn't know it. "We exercised the power of women," she said, "long before it had a name." (Courtesy of the *Detroit Free Press*; photograph by Pauline Lubens.)

Sr. Carol (Laura) Quigley was the IHM president from 1982 to 1988. She also was president of the Leadership Council of Women Religious (LCWR). She worked in Recife, Brazil, for five years. She stopped wearing habits because, she told an interviewer, "they establish a distance." She also was a coordinator of leadership development for the Core City Neighborhoods agency in Detroit and a vice president of Marygrove College. When she died unexpectedly in 2019 at the age of 78, she was program coordinator for River House Spirituality Center in Monroe.

Seven

WHERE THERE IS A NEED

Redemptorist priest Rev. Louis Gillet, the Monroe IHMs cofounder, was a Belgian missionary to settlements in 1840s Michigan. "I desire to be everywhere when I see so many needs," he said of his work. That, too, has inspired the IHMs. Since 1969, IHMs have worked with the disadvantaged in Ghana, South Africa, Kenya, Uganda, and Zimbabwe. In December 2000, several IHMs met in Uganda. From left to right in the front row are Srs. Ann (Ann Arthur) Aseltyne, Annette (Madonna Marie) St. Amour, Susan Rakoczy, Marie-Esther Haflett, and Joan (Robert Jean) Mumaw. Behind them are Srs. Peg (Cornelia) O'Shea (left) and Judith (John Vincent) Coyle. Their ministries have been examples of IHMs in action whether they were oceans away or on the street marching to make a difference.

In 1948, the Monroe IHMs dispatched several sisters to open a mission in Cayey, Puerto Rico, about 25 miles from San Juan. It was the congregation's first mission outside the continental United States. IHMs eventually opened four schools in Puerto Rico.

Mother Teresa McGivney (at center in the dark habit) was the congregation's general superior when she visited with IHM teaching sisters posted to Puerto Rico. They wore white habits to better cope with the island heat. Because of the influence of their IHM teachers, several women from Puerto Rico joined the congregation.

In the 1960s, Detroit cardinal John Dearden asked the IHMs to provide sisters for a mission evangelization team to staff a parish in Recife, in the northeast of Brazil along the Atlantic Ocean. "Many of the people around us did not have running water or electricity" and lived in mud houses, recalled Sr. Dorothy (Mary Seton) Diederichs (at left in the first row).

On August 28, 1969, IHM Sisters arrived in Masaka, Uganda. Their hosts, in the first row, were Mother Stanislaus (left) and Mother Vincent of the Bannabikira Sisters. The four IHMs were, from left to right in the second row, Srs. Anna Marie Grix, Anne Marie (Charles Borromeo) Hughes, Jane (Marmion) Johnson, and Julia (Mary Carmen) Seim. The photograph was taken by another IHM, Sr. Ellen (Berchmans) Balle.

In February 1986, St. Anne parish leaders bestowed a sheep named Monroe on IHM Sisters who had arrived months earlier to teach in the South African township of Mpophomeni. The sheep was later served for Easter dinner. Seated are, from left to right, Srs. Judith Coyle, former IHM Eileen Karrer, and Srs. Annette Boyle, Annette St. Amour, and Joan Mumaw.

In April 1994, for the first time, South Africa held free elections in which any citizen, regardless of race, could vote. It marked the end of the apartheid government. IHMs were volunteer election monitors. Pictured from left to right are Srs. Susan Rakoczy, Judith Coyle, Annette St. Amour, Rita (Marie Ambrose) Rennell, Peg O'Shea, and former IHM Eileen Karrer.

Srs. Rose Graham (left) and Genevieve (William Joseph) Petrak meet with Harare, Zimbabwe, bishop Patrick Fani Chakaipa in January 1993.

Srs. Ann (Ann Arthur) Aseltyne, back left, and Joan (Robert Jean) Mumaw meet with friends in Ghana. Sister Ann taught at teacher-training colleges in Ghana, South Africa, and Uganda. Sr. Joan Mumaw heads a Baltimore-based nonprofit, Friends in Solidarity, focused on raising funds for education and training programs in South Sudan.

In February 1998, several IHMs gathered for a weekend of reflection in the Drakensburg Mountains in the Orange Free State, South Africa. In the first row are, from left to right, Srs. Judith Coyle and Annette St. Amour. In the second row are Srs. Joan Mumaw, Peg O'Shea, Susan Rakoczy, Mary Ann (John Andrew) Markel (who was visiting from Monroe), and Mary (Mary Bede) Kinney.

IHM Sr. Susan Rakoczy (left) has taught in South Africa for more than 30 years. She is a theologian and the author of books that explore women's contributions to Christian theology, especially those of African women. Here, she is pictured with one of her students at St. Joseph's Theological Institute in Cedara, South Africa.

At home, IHMs have committed themselves to purposeful action. In the 1980s, they participated in a large march calling for peace.

As the United States went to war against Iraq in 2003, the IHMs marched for peace in Monroe.

For 12 years, including 7 as director, Sr. Gloria Rivera helmed Freedom House, a temporary sanctuary for immigrants seeking asylum in the United States because of persecution in their native countries. Freedom House, located in Detroit, provides food, shelter, education, and assistance to these survivors of persecution.

Sr. Elizabeth (John Raphael) Walters has gone to jail at least a dozen times to promote peace. In this 1986 photograph, she was serving six months in a Michigan county jail for trespassing on a Michigan Air Force base after she'd been banned for previous protests to draw attention to the proliferation of nuclear weapons. (Courtesy of the *Detroit Free Press*; photograph by Alan Kamuda.)

IHMs participate in a protest at the US Army School of the Americas, now called the Western Hemisphere Institute for Security Cooperation. The Georgia facility enrolls members of foreign militaries who are allies of the United States. Protesters believe the training has helped repressive regimes stay in power.

IHMs participate in the annual AIDS Walk. From left to right are Srs. Elizabeth (John Raphael) Walters, Margaret (Kevin Mary) Hughes, Mary Ann (Madeleine Marie) Ford, and Marie Cyril Delisi.

The Nuns on the Bus movement got its start in the 2012 presidential election year. It was cofounded by Sr. Simone Campbell, who has led the Catholic social justice lobby called NETWORK and is a member of the Sisters of Social Services congregation. For many years, IHM Sr. Nancy Sylvester worked for NETWORK. Nuns on the Bus traveled to many cities to highlight national issues and how elected officials can do more to help the poor and working class. IHMs turned out to welcome the Nuns on the Bus at one of the group's past visits.

In 2015, Sr. Margaret (Mary Hofbauer) Alandt participated in the 50th anniversary of Bloody Sunday, when armed police beat civil rights demonstrators as they marched from Selma to the Alabama state capitol in Montgomery. She attended, in part, to honor the journey of another IHM, Sr. Shirley (Mary Gerald) Ellis, who devoted her life to social justice. Sister Shirley was one of only five women religious from the Archdiocese of Detroit to participate in the Selma-to-Montgomery Civil Rights March in 1965.

Eight

THE SUSTAINABLE MOTHERHOUSE

The IHM Motherhouse in Monroe underwent a $56-million renovation from 2001 to 2003. The project epitomized the sisters' commitment to environmental awareness and sustainability. "Our mission is to serve the poor and abandoned . . . and the Earth has really been abandoned," Sr. Janet (Ann Rita) Ryan, a member of the IHM Leadership Council at the time, told the *Toledo Blade* in 2002. She and other hard-hatted members of the IHM team pose on the Motherhouse grounds under a crane as the renovation commences in 2001. In 2000, the IHMs made a commitment "to develop and act out of an ecological consciousness, individually and corporately. Specifically, this means . . . collaborating with others in shaping public policies that will foster ecological co-responsibility and eco-justice."

The IHM Leadership Council during the renovation included, from left to right, Srs. Frances Mlocek, Anne Crimmins, Paula Cooney, Janet Ryan, Virginia Pfau, Mary Katherine Hamilton, Carolyn Campbell, and Barbara Weigand. In the aerial photograph below, construction equipment is rearranging the 280-acre campus. The Motherhouse complex is at center left. The Motherhouse's 243 sisters had to leave their living quarters and move into the empty St. Mary Academy (on the right in the image), which had been a boarding school for girls until it closed in 1986.

The interior was taken down to the 18-inch brick and stone walls. The photograph at right shows where a four-story staircase previously stood. It cost about $150 per square foot to ecologically modernize the Motherhouse. The staggering sum was twice the initial estimate. When IHMs convened a meeting about the undertaking, sisters broke out into small groups of 15. In one group, sisters wondered how they could raise the money and threw in what cash they had on them; they amassed $150. "Here's the first square foot," Sr. Marie Gabriel Hungerman later told the congregation as hundreds of IHMs cheered. It was popular for alumnae and others to make a $150 donation.

The Motherhouse landscape now helps recycle water. Water from sinks and showers inside are routed to a holding tank, where solids are filtered out. Then, it flows into the shallow marsh, pond, and meadow, where water is directed back to the Motherhouse toilets. The three-acre wetlands recycle about 40 percent of the building's water. (Courtesy of SMP Architects and Halkin Mason Photography.)

The Motherhouse's signature statue of Mary underwent masonry repair. The renovation architects were Susan Maxman & Partners, now SMP Architects. The renovation was honored by the American Institute of Architects in 2006. A key component of the renovation is a geothermal heating and cooling system and structures that recycle heat from exhaust systems.

Carpenter Gary Durall worked on the 450 doors that were refinished. He told the *Detroit Free Press*: "The sisters taught me all throughout grade school. It's good to be here." Period light fixtures were rewired, and old bathroom stalls, made of marble, were recut for window sills. (Courtesy of the *Detroit Free Press*; photograph by Amy Leang.)

Work crews often met under the stained-glass windows of the Motherhouse chapel. Siblings (and Sisters) Jean (Eymarda) and Mary (Coronata) Laubacher would address new crews, asking God to bless the workers, their families, and their tools, and sprinkle them with holy water. They also distributed rules prohibiting loud radios and cussing. The renovation also prompted the IHMs to create the River Raisin Institute in 2003. The institute sponsors educational programming "to respect, nurture and promote the well-being of all creation," according to its website (www.rriearth.org).

Sr. Marjorie (Ann Gregory) McFarland relaxes in her new bedroom, with private bath, in the renovated Motherhouse. It was a world of difference from when she entered the IHMs and was assigned to a bunk in a room with 12 other women and shared a dormitory bathroom.

The renovation of the Motherhouse won multiple awards. The Motherhouse entrance is shown here. Since 2003, more than 10,000 visitors, including classes from colleges and universities, have taken the IHM Green House tour. (Courtesy of SMP Architects and Halkin Mason Photography.)

The IHMs have leased a portion of the Motherhouse complex to DTE Energy, the utility formerly known as Detroit Edison. Solar energy panels cover a wide swath of land. In the 1970s and 1980s, IHMs were a steady presence at stockholder meetings to press the utility about safety issues. In 2012, IHM president Sr. Mary Jane Herb cut the ribbon for the solar panel field.

Sr. James Marian Sarchet builds these boxes for IHM Sisters who elect cremation upon their deaths. A cremation box is shown here against the backdrop of a courtyard at the Motherhouse filled with personalized pavers purchased by friends and families of IHM Sisters. (Photograph by Patricia Montemurri.)

More than 1,546 IHM Sisters are buried in Monroe. In the congregation's early years, sisters were buried at the public St. Joseph Cemetery. Adjacent to it is St. Mary Cemetery, in use since 1889 and where each sister's resting place is marked with a simple square gravestone. (Photograph by Diane Weiss.)

There is an organic farm behind the Motherhouse. Here, Sr. Anne (Michael Ann) Wisda harvests tomatoes from her patch ringed with non-GMO heirloom zinnias. The two-acre community garden began in 1998. Plots and raised beds are available for lease. Some of the organic harvest supports a local food pantry. The community garden, directed by Bob Dluzen, also runs a program to teach gardening to people recently released from jail. (Photograph by Patricia Montemurri.)

Nine

IHMs in Action Today

These faces represent the women who call themselves Sisters, Servants of the Immaculate Heart of Mary. They were among 300 IHM Sisters and Associates who gathered in Monroe in July 2019 to review, reconnect, and pray at the congregation's annual assembly. Pictured are, from left to right, Srs. Sandrita Poupart Valentin, Maria Antonia Aranda Diaz, Maxine Kollasch, Jane Aseltyne, Julie Vieira, and Audra Turnbull. Their ministries offer a sample of what IHMs do and who they are today. Sister Sandrita came to the congregation from her native Puerto Rico, where IHMs taught her and where she has taught elementary and special education in San Juan. Sister Maria Antonia ministers in Juarez, Mexico, considered one of the world's most violent cities, which is across the border from El Paso, Texas; her work, along with that of several other IHMs, is part of a 40-year ministry by the IHMs in Mexico. Sisters Maxine and Julie cofounded A Nun's Life Ministry, an online outreach that features podcasts, blogs, interactive forums, and other social media centered on religious life. Sisters Jane and Audra are among the newest and youngest IHMs, adept at deploying digital media to inspire others with their own spiritual journeys. Sister Jane's extended family includes two great-aunts who became IHMs. Sister Audra grew up in Missouri and learned about the IHMs from Googling "nuns" and landing on A Nun's Life Ministry; she has worked with Compassionate Companions/Monroe County Guardians, acting as a public guardian for adults with developmental and mental health challenges. (Photograph by Michaela Kotanova.)

The IHM Sisters Leadership Council (in office until 2024) includes, from left to right, Srs. Margaret Chapman, Patricia (Ann Bernard) McCluskey, Pres. Mary Jane Herb, Ellen Rinke, and Marianne Gaynor. "The Sisters, Servants of the Immaculate Heart of Mary stand strong on our foundation that began on November 10, 1845. We look forward to the future knowing that we are grounded in deep faith, have a courageous spirit and will continue to act for justice," wrote Sister Mary Jane as the 175th anniversary year commenced. "Our foundation is grounded in the deep faith of our cofounders, Theresa Maxis, IHM, and Louis Florent Gillet, CSsR. Throughout 175 years, deep faith has guided us. Following the Second Vatican Council, we answered God's call and ventured into various ministries. Besides teaching, the IHM Sisters began serving the people of God as parish ministers, social workers, in the areas of spirituality, jail ministry and others, always attentive to the poor and vulnerable. Looking to the future, despite being a smaller community, we will continue to join with our associates and co-ministers, grounded in the Gospel message, to live the IHM mission in new ways. Through the years, courageous spirit has galvanized us. Embarking on construction of our Motherhouse during the Depression took a courageous spirit. The call to serve in Puerto Rico, Brazil, Honduras, Africa, and Mexico challenged us to move beyond our borders. We stood with the people in South Africa as they faced apartheid. In 2000, we renovated our Motherhouse with ecologically sustainable features to demonstrate care for Earth and consideration for those who will come after us. Our IHM Constitutions challenge us 'to eradicate the causes of injustice and oppression and to help create structures that will promote justice and peace and bring unity among all peoples.' We have made a particular commitment to be attentive to the poor and the vulnerable in the city of Detroit. Through our Peace, Justice and Sustainability Office, we respond to political challenges with public statements to address the injustices within our society. We are rooted in our rich history, focused on the future and united in the fires ignited by our founders 175 years ago."

Founded by IHMs in 2006, A Nun's Life Ministry and its interactive website, ANunsLife.org, can provide answers to questions about religious life. Since 2009, its podcasts have been downloaded more than 1 million times. Srs. Julie Vieira (right) and Maxine Kollasch (left) cofounded the ministry as they both studied to become IHMs. Sister Julie's blog about her journey went viral because of her honest discussion of her yearning for religious life—and also her taste for beer. Sister Julie is now the program director for the IHM Spirituality Centers in metro Detroit. Sister Maxine is the executive director of A Nun's Life Ministry and the host of the *Ask Sister* podcast; more than 1,000 podcasts, featuring a wide range of Catholic luminaries, have been produced and downloaded. Through social media, A Nun's Life Ministry has reached people in over 150 countries. Sr. Audra Turnbull (center) found answers to some of her questions about religious life while following the *A Nun's Life* blog and then working for the ministry. She took her first vows to become an IHM in 2018. These women have been pioneers in using the Internet and social media to reinvigorate religious practice in the digital age. They also take their show on the road, visiting and broadcasting from convents, motherhouses, and monasteries across the country. (Photograph by Diane Weiss.)

Open the door to the Maxis Spirituality Center in the downriver Detroit suburb of Riverview, and serenity awaits. "Enter the Quiet," reads the sign greeting visitors who come for retreats, spiritual counseling, and workshops to learn more about practices such as contemplative prayer. Sr. Lynne Moldenhauer (pictured) runs the center for the IHMs. A onetime South Carolina probation and parole officer, she sometimes plays the guitar during workshops. (Photograph by Patricia Montemurri.)

River House, just steps away from the River Raisin in Monroe, was built in 1936 and originally was the rectory for the priests who led services at the IHM Motherhouse just across West Elm Avenue. In the 1980s, it was converted to the IHM Novitiate residence for women who were novices and studying to become vowed sisters. Since 2009, it's been known as River House, a place for renewal that offers seminars, study groups, and one-on-one spiritual direction. (Photograph by Molly Hunt.)

River House visitors enjoy a day at the water's edge. It offers spiritual counseling and retreat space for individuals and small groups. Staff and friends gather on the porch outside the house with the River Raisin behind them. (Photograph by Molly Hunt.)

Visitation Spirituality Center, located on the Marian High School grounds in Bloomfield Hills, offers multiple programs and events. Sr. Marie (Marie George) Miller, IHM, seated at far right, offers an opening prayer for the Musings over Mugs gathering, held on the first Saturday of every month. From left to right are Michele Dragisity, Cindy Bailey, Michele Matuszewski, IHM Associate B.J. Schlachter, Visitation director Sr. Kathleen Budesky, and coordinator Sr. Angela Cerna-Plata. (Photograph by Patricia Montemurri.)

It's a new ministry for the IHMs. In 2017, from left to right, Srs. Agnes (Gerarda) Anderson, Angela Therese Meram, and Susan Mahalik launched this ministry that supplies communion bread to parishes in Michigan, Ohio, Indiana, New York, and Kentucky.

The IHM Motherhouse Gift Shop is open from 10:00 a.m. to 2:00 p.m. Tuesday through Thursday and for special events. Purchases of fair-trade crafts and other items benefit female entrepreneurs in developing countries. In the foreground is Sr. Gail (John Maureen) Addis. In the back is Sr. Roberta Richmond. (Photograph by Patricia Montemurri.)

The IHMs employ some 225 full- and part-time employees at their Monroe campus, many of them in the health care field, to ensure quality, round-the-clock care for sisters and other residents in their long-term facilities. The sisters design programs and seminars so employees can learn more about the congregation's history and goals. Here, IHM employees pose on the Motherhouse steps for a 2019 recruiting campaign. From left to right are Angela O'Rourke, Kim Dusseau, Nikki Schnebele, Brian Lochner, Stephen Light, and JoAnne Lietaert. (Photograph by Molly Hunt.)

Sr. Brigid Mary Wade leads a group of sixth-graders from throughout Monroe County during the Lake Erie Water Festival in May 2019. (Photograph by Michaela Kotanova.)

The IHM Archives holds photographs and biographical files of nearly 2,000 IHM Sisters. Among the holdings are the doctoral dissertations of 82 IHMs. Archives staffers past and present gathered in October 2019. Pictured here are, from left to right, (first row) Srs. Diann Cousino, Shirley Houff, Marie André Walsh, Joan Glisky, and former archivist Donna Westley; (second row) Srs. Anne Crane, Marie Clark, Margaret Babcock, Rita Fisher, Fran Pokriefka, and Fran Mlocek; (third row) archives assistant Deborah Saul and archivist Jennifer Meacham. (Photograph by Patricia Montemurri.)

Sr. Kathleen Onderbeke is the pastoral administrator at Ss. Francis and Clare Parish in Birch Run, near Flint, Michigan. Like many IHMs, she began her ministry as a K–12 teacher. She's also served as the director of Faith Formation at St. Louis Parish in Clinton Township, Michigan. In 2018, she began work in this small Saginaw County parish with rural roots, where her work is diverse and even includes pinch-hitting with the tractor lawn mower. (Photograph by D. Hamilton.)

IHMs represent! There were 13,000 athletes at the 2019 National Senior Games in Albuquerque, New Mexico, in 2019, and IHMs were among them. From left to right are IHM Associate Jan Mignano and Srs. Loretta (Vincent de Paul) Schroeder, Theresa (John Christopher) Fix, and Margaret Chapman. Sister Theresa competed in basketball. The other three could be found on the golf course.

Sr. Beth (Marie Alma) Wood took up running in her 50s. In her 80s, she completed at least one full marathon each year. During her years of ministry, she worked at the Vatican Library. Her training includes a three-mile loop around the Motherhouse complex. She runs with determination to feel the elation and exhaustion of crossing the finish line. On October 20, 2019, at age 90, she was the last of 1,541 runners in the *Detroit Free Press*/TCF Bank International Half-Marathon, finishing the 13.1 miles in 5:17:45. (Photograph by Patricia Montemurri.)

For 21 years, Sr. Sharon (Marie Russell) Holland was one of the highest-ranking women to work at the Vatican. Sister Sharon, pictured here in her Vatican office in 2005, is a canon lawyer and an expert in Catholic Church law regarding priests, nuns, and sisters. As president of the Leadership Conference of Women Religious (LCWR) in 2014–2015, she negotiated the end of the Vatican's doctrinal assessment of the LCWR, initiated under Pope Benedict XVI and resolved under Pope Francis. The Vatican investigation into American sisters was initiated in part because some bishops believed some US congregations of women religious, such as the IHMs, had become too liberal in their support of social justice issues. (Courtesy of the *Detroit Free Press*; photograph by Romain Blanquart.)

Sr. Sandra Marie (John Gregory) Schneiders has published several books, including *Prophets in Their Own Country: Women Religious Bearing Witness to the Gospel in a Troubled Church*. Her work has been internationally recognized and honored. She holds a doctorate degree in sacred theology from the Pontifical Gregorian University in Rome. She is a professor emerita in the Jesuit School of Theology at the Graduate Theological Union in Berkeley, California. As an IHM, "I have been able to do with my life what I most wanted to do: seek God, live and preach the Gospel," she said in 2016. "Religion has been the single greatest interest in my life since I was a little kid. I have been able to pursue that interest in the company of others who had the same desires."

The IHMs are transforming a wing of the Motherhouse into a senior living complex that is open to the public. In 2019, an initial 19 units were available for purchase. Floor plans include one-and two-bedroom units, with balconies, ranging from $82,900 to $146,800. To learn more, visit www.ihmslc. org or call (734) 240-8230.

IHM Senior Living Community includes units for independent and assisted care living, memory care, and skilled nursing services. It has consistently received five-star ratings from Medicare. Volunteers are always welcome to visit and assist residents, as Kay Wiseman (right) did while chatting with Sr. Antoinette (Jean Claire) McNamara.

Several IHM Sisters attended a Detroit protest in July 2019 against US policies separating parents from children as Central American families fleeing violence sought asylum at the Mexico-Texas border. IHM Sisters offer pastoral care to men detained by US immigration agents at a Monroe detention center. Pictured here are, from left to right, Srs. Elizabeth (John Raphael) Walters, Judith (Marie Jude) O'Brien, and Margaret (Kevin Mary) Hughes. (Photograph by Thom Mann.)

IHMs work in Juarez, Mexico, across the border from El Paso, Texas. In January 2019, several Monroe IHMs visited to help IHMs aiding asylum-seekers. Pictured in front are Srs. Julie Vieira (left) and Angela Cerna-Plata. Behind them are, from left to right, Srs. Carmen Armenta Lara, Marie Antonia Aranda Diaz, Judith Bonini, and Maureen Kelly. (Courtesy of Sr. Julie Vieira.)

Srs. Mary Bea Keeley (left) and Judith (Norma Jean) Kaiser are glad to see each other at the July 2019 assembly at the IHM Motherhouse in Monroe. (Photograph by Michaela Kotanova.)

From left to right, Srs. Monica (Marie Monica) Stuhlreyer, Amata Miller, Anne (Michael Ann) Wisda, and Carolina (Esperanza) Diez de Andino welcome participants with song. (Photograph by Michaela Kotanova.)

Sr. Judith (Ann Raymond) Bonini exults at assembly. Sister Judith has been an elementary-school teacher, a pastoral associate working with parishes in Saginaw, a hospital chaplain, and a spiritual director. (Photograph by Michaela Kotanova.)

Sr. Carmen Armenta Lara, who ministers in Juarez, Mexico, couldn't make it to the 2019 Jubilee to mark her 25th year as an IHM. But friends raised a glass in her honor over a photograph of her. Sister Carmen first met IHMs at a Bible study in Juarez and was the first woman from Mexico to join the congregation. She has worked among the poor in Mexico. "Each sister received me with open arms and so much love," she says, "and gave me the confidence to feel I belonged." (Photograph by Molly Hunt.)

To collect their thoughts, IHMs put them in a basket. At far left is Sr. Angela Hibbard, next to Sr. Anita Pfieffer. At right is Sr. Barbara Northrup. (Photograph by Michaela Kotanova.)

Sr. Angela Therese Meram bangs the drum for the start of the Jubilee Mass in the Motherhouse chapel celebrating IHMs' milestone anniversaries. To the left of Sister Angela is Sr. Marylyn (Peter Faber) Russ, and to the right is Sr. Patricia Nagle, who is being greeted by Sr. Rosemary (Mary Assunta) Cassar. (Photograph by Molly Hunt.)

Sr. Charlotte Walby, age 102, leads Jubilarians into the Motherhouse chapel in July 2019. Jubilarians are sisters celebrating milestone anniversaries of their reception into the IHM congregation. Jubilarians are celebrated at anniversaries for 25, 50, 60, 70, 75, and 80 years of IHM service.

Celebrating 60 years as IHMs in July 2019 are, from left to right, (first row) Srs. Frances (Peter Damian) Mlocek, Nancy Lee (Philippine) Smith, Jean (Ann Christopher) Booms, and Margaret (Kevin Mary) Hughes; (second row) Srs. Angela Therese Meram, Patricia Nagle, Margaret (Kathleen Marie) Sweeney, Marylyn (Peter Faber) Russ, Angela Cerna-Plata, Agnes (Gerarda) Anderson, and Rose Graham. (Photograph by Molly Hunt.)

Celebrating 70 years as IHMs in July 2019 are, from left to right, Srs. Margaret (Margaret Leo) Canuelle, Therese (James Marie) Kearney, Grace Mary Olfs, and Theresa (Bonaventure) Tenbusch. (Photograph by Molly Hunt.)

Celebrating 75 years as IHMs in July 2019 are, from left to right, (first row) Srs. Marietta Murphy, Antoinette (Jean Clare) McNamara, and Remi (Mary Remi) Pauwels; (second row) Srs. Janet Sullivan, Alys (Gerontia) Currier, and Marguerite (Edwarda) Gibbs. (Photograph by Molly Hunt.)

Sr. Diane Brown took her final vows to become an IHM on July 29, 2019, at the Sacred Heart Chapel of Marygrove College in Detroit. She was widowed in 2005 and moved to Detroit to work as the coordinator of Marygrove College's Master in the Art of Teaching program. In coming to know IHM Sisters, she was drawn to a religious vocation. She converted to Catholicism and enrolled in Scripture and theology classes. Above, she is accompanied on her way into the chapel by Sr. Suzanne (Marie Peter) Sattler (right). Behind them are Srs. Mary Jane Herb (left) and Ellen Rinke. Below, Sister Diane makes her final vows in front of the altar. (Both, photograph by Molly Hunt.)

Janice Mignano speaks at the August 18, 2019, Mass in which she became an IHM Associate. Associates are laypeople—men or women, single or married, and of varied faith backgrounds—who share the IHMs' values and goals. Mignano learned about the IHMs' ministries when she golfed in the annual Royal Blue Classic tournaments (a fundraiser for the IHMs). To the left are Srs. Peggy (Margarita) Schmidt (far left) and Patricia (Ann Bernard) McCluskey (next to Mignano). To the right is IHM Associates co-coordinator Barbara Bacci Yugovich. (Photograph by Molly Hunt.)

When Sarah Nash became an IHM Associate, her husband, Kevin, and daughters Magdelene (right) and Evelyn celebrated with her. Nash is the coordinator of the IHM Justice, Peace, and Sustainability Office. She partnered with Sr. Mary Ann (Marie Ann) Flanagan for spiritual direction before making a commitment to become an IHM Associate on September 22, 2019. (Photograph by Patricia Montemurri.)

These are some of the 120 IHM Associates who made a commitment to share in the life and ministry of the IHM community. Under a framework of spiritual guidance, associates align themselves with the IHM spirit, mission, and values. "Associates maintain their own homes, families and lifestyles. After a period of discernment and orientation, they enter into a formal covenant with the community for a specific, renewable period of time, focusing on prayer, community and ministry," according to the IHMs. From left to right are (first row) Kate Keever, Marsha West, and Nancy Coman; (second row) Frank McAuliffe, Barbara Bacci Yugovich, Sharon Carolin, Jan Mignano, Charles Van Vleet, Barbara Jennings, and Mary Conner. (Photograph by Molly Hunt.)

This box sits in the IHM Motherhouse Chapel. It holds memorial prayer cards for deceased IHMs. The small slips of paper carry the names of the nearly 1,600 IHMs who have passed away since the congregation's founding in 1845. IHM Sisters who attend Mass pick up a slip and offer prayers in memory. On one slip is the name of IHM Sr. Ann (Ann Arthur) Aseltyne, who died at the age of 92 on October 23, 2018. Just a few months later, Sister Ann's great-niece, Jane Aseltyne, took vows to become an IHM. (Photograph by Patricia Montemurri.)

On August 4, 2019, Jane Aseltyne, age 34, took vows to become an IHM at the Motherhouse chapel. Her great-aunt, IHM Sr. Patricia Aseltyne, accompanied her, as shown above. Two of Sister Jane's aunts, Patricia and the late Ann Aseltyne, became IHM Sisters. Their ministries and counsel, in part, guided her to this day. Below, she makes her first vows as IHM congregation president Sr. Mary Jane Herb stands to her right and Sr. Marjorie (Katherine Drexel) Polys stands to her left. Celebrating Mass is Rev. Robert Schramm. (Both, photograph by Diane Weiss.)

Above, a community of faith extends hands out to bless the new IHM, Sr. Jane Aseltyne. Below, Sister Jane wears a plain band on her finger extending a tradition of women religious wearing such rings to signify their commitment to Jesus rather than a spouse. As Sister Jane prepared to become an IHM over a four-year process, she worked with the online IHM ministry, ANunsLife. org. This is how Sister Jane responded to one woman's queries: "Be open with God, ask God questions, and let God know how you're feeling. God will always be walking with you and guiding your path. Being married and having a family is [a] different call than to religious life. So perhaps you can make a list of what attracts you to each kind of lifestyle, then sit with that list in prayer. You might be surprised at what surfaces! Also, if you have the chance, I'd recommend getting to know some sisters in your area." (Both, photograph by Diane Weiss.)

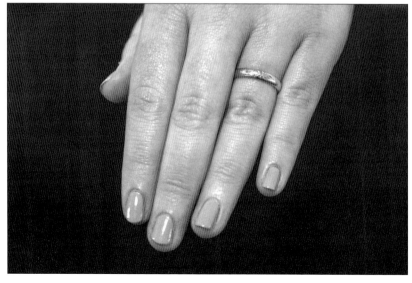

Sr. Jane Aseltyne is congratulated by friends after taking her vows. In the fall of 2019, she began pursuing theological studies at the Catholic Theological Union in Chicago. (Both, photograph by Diane Weiss.)

Sr. Jane Aseltyne proceeds out of the IHM Motherhouse Chapel minutes after she made vows as the newest member of the Sisters, Servants of the Immaculate Heart of Mary. (Photograph by Diane Weiss.)

On November 9, 2019, the IHM Sisters marked the start of their 175th anniversary year with a Founder's Day Mass and cake at the Motherhouse in Monroe. From left to right are Srs. Patricia (Helen Mary) Aseltyne, June (Richardine) Johnson, Paula (Marie Paula) Cooney, Mary Jane Herb, Nancy Sylvester, Brigid (Brigid Mary) Wade, Beth (Marie Alma) Wood, and Betty (Marie Nicholas) Leon. Since the congregation's founding in 1845, the IHM landmark campus has evolved and endured. When visitors enter the Motherhouse, this sign proclaims the congregation's values and goals.

BIBLIOGRAPHY

Kelley, Sr. Rosalita. *Achievement of a Century: The Motherhouse and Missions.* Detroit: Evans, Winter, Hebb, 1948.

———. *No Greater Service: The History of the Congregation of the Sisters, Servants of the Immaculate Heart of Mary, Monroe, Michigan, 1845–1945.* Detroit: Evans, Winter, Hebb, 1948.

Maher, Mary Jo, IHM. *A Compelling Vision: History of the IHM Overseas Missions.* Monroe, MI: Sisters, Servants of the Immaculate Heart of Mary, 2000.

Sisters, Servants of The Immaculate Heart of Mary. *Building Sisterhood: A Feminist History of the Sisters, Servants of the Immaculate Heart of Mary.* Syracuse, NY: Syracuse University Press, 1997.

Vinyard, JoEllen. *For Faith and Fortune: The Education of Catholic Immigrants in Detroit, 1805–1925.* Chicago: University of Illinois Press, 1998.

ABOUT THE SISTERS, SERVANTS OF THE IMMACULATE HEART OF MARY

The ministries of the Sisters, Servants of the Immaculate Heart of Mary change people's lives.

If you were taught by an IHM and know her only by her religious name (before many IHMs switched to using their original birth names), it may be possible to identify and contact her through the IHM website, www.ihmsisters.org. The life stories of many IHMs—those who are alive and those who have died—are available on the website, which is also accessible in Spanish. The website also features videos of several sisters delivering book reviews and a list of recommended readings.

The IHMs also take prayer requests via the website. Masses in the Motherhouse Chapel are open to the public. Check the website for Mass times.

The IHMs depend on volunteers for assistance with driving sisters to appointments and assisting residents with correspondence and email, reading, recreational activities, and arts and crafts.

To learn about becoming an IHM Sister, contact Sr. Candyce (Lauren) Rekart at (734) 240-9820 or email her at crekart@ihmsisters.org. Do a search for the "Virtual Discernment Retreat" on the IHM website for a guide.

To learn about the IHM Associates initiative for laypeople, contact Associates co-coordinators Sr. Anne (Judith Mary) Crimmins and Barbara Bacci Yugovich at (734) 240-9672 or email acrimmins@ihmsisters.org or byugovich@ihmsisters.org.

The IHMs are transforming a wing of the Motherhouse into a Life Plan Community, starting with 19 apartments available for purchase by members of the public. Floor plans include one-bedroom and two-bedroom units with balconies, with prices ranging from $82,900 to $146,800. To learn more, visit www.ihmslc.org or call (734) 240-8230.

Tours of the Motherhouse may be arranged by calling (734) 240-9754 or emailing svenier@ihmsisters.org. Motherhouse facilities also are available for rentals, for events such as conferences and weddings, and can accommodate groups of 15 to 250 people.

The IHM Sisters depend on donations to help support their ministries and to fund retirement and housing costs. The IHM Retirement Fund assists with health care for IHMs. The IHM Ministry Fund supports IHMs as they fulfill their work with the disadvantaged and promote social justice and human rights. The IHM Overseas and Missions Fund supports the ministries of IHMs abroad. You may also contribute to the IHM's Area of Greatest Need Fund, which allows the sisters to use the donation at their discretion.

Donations are accepted at ihmsisters.org under the "Ways of Contributing" tab. Checks can be mailed to the IHM Sisters Development Office at 610 West Elm Avenue, Monroe, Michigan, 48162-7909. For more information, call the IHM Development Office at (734) 240-9860.

DISCOVER THOUSANDS OF LOCAL HISTORY BOOKS
FEATURING MILLIONS OF VINTAGE IMAGES

Arcadia Publishing, the leading local history publisher in the United States, is committed to making history accessible and meaningful through publishing books that celebrate and preserve the heritage of America's people and places.

Find more books like this at
www.arcadiapublishing.com

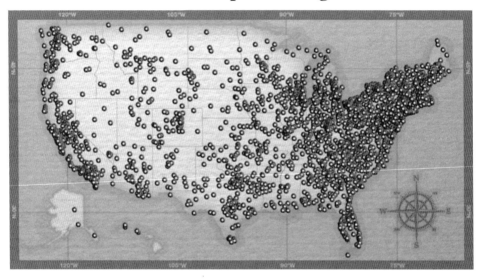

Search for your hometown history, your old stomping grounds, and even your favorite sports team.

Consistent with our mission to preserve history on a local level, this book was printed in South Carolina on American-made paper and manufactured entirely in the United States. Products carrying the accredited Forest Stewardship Council (FSC) label are printed on 100 percent FSC-certified paper.

MADE IN THE USA